Apartment Alchemy

50 Ways Small Apartment Owners Can Boost Their Cash Flow and Wealth

By Lance A. Edwards

Copyright © 2023 by Lance A. Edwards and
First Cornerstone Group, LLC

All rights reserved. No part of this publication may be reproduced, distributed, or transmitted in any form or by any means, including photocopying, recording, or other electronic or mechanical methods, without the prior written permission of the publisher, except in the case of brief quotations embodied in critical reviews and certain other noncommercial uses permitted by copyright law. For permission requests, write to the publisher, addressed "Attention: Permissions Coordinator," at the address below.

First Cornerstone Group, LLC
14825 St. Mary's Lane, Suite 260
Houston, TX 77079
713-476-0102
ClientCare@fcgllc.com

This publication is designed to provide accurate and authoritative information with regard to the subject matter covered. It is sold with the understanding that the publisher is not engaged in rendering legal, accounting, or other professional advice. If legal advice or other expert assistance is required, the services of a competent professional person should be sought.

The author, Lance Edwards, is available for a limited number of speaking engagements and consulting assignments. He also has a selection of training programs and mentoring programs. For information, contact Lance Edwards at 713-476-0102 or ClientCare@fcgllc.com

Dedication

This book is first dedicated to my grandfather, A. Tillis Edwards, Jr., who – through his life – inspired me into entrepreneurship. A living example of the self-made man, he, and many entrepreneurs like him, collaborated to build an industry – the Florida Citrus industry. During the writing of this book, he was posthumously inducted into the Florida Citrus Hall of Fame.

Finally, I wish to dedicate this book to all the mentors, partners, team members, and clients who have enabled the principles in this book to not only be organized and tested but realized – proving that anyone can do it.

Table of Contents

Dedication v

Chapter 1: Introduction 1

Chapter 2: The Base Metals 3

Chapter 3: Fantastical Formulas 19

Chapter 4: Powerful Potions 39

Chapter 5: Valuable Variations 63

Chapter 6: Why Small Apartments Are The Ideal Investment 81

Chapter 7: Summary Of Resources And Offers 91

Chapter 8: About The Author 95

Disclaimer 99

Chapter 1

Introduction

"Indeed, I am as skilled as any alchemist, but instead of turning lead into gold, I turn my fear into daring, and assuredly that is a far greater trick."

– Robin LaFevers

Alchemy, in some form or another, has been practiced for nearly two millennia, beginning in China and India in the first and second centuries. Alchemy as we envision it – wizened sages in velvet robes and cone-shaped hats toiling away over bubbling beakers in darkened crypts – flourished in the Middle Ages between 1000 and 1500 AD.

Drawing upon beliefs reaching back to Aristotle and the early Greek philosophers, alchemists sought perfection primarily by transforming "inferior" metals into what they considered the perfect metal – gold. Their belief in gold's perfection may have sprung from the fact it doesn't rust or tarnish (or maybe simply because you could buy a lot of cool stuff with it!).

Interestingly, the alchemists believed that nature existed in a cycle of self-perfection and that all those inferior metals would eventually reach "gold status." Their efforts, therefore, were to simply speed up the process in a laboratory. In other words, "Forget waiting! Let's get to the gold!"

So, what does this have to do with you and me and real estate investing?

Let's imagine that all real estate investments are lead. Like lead they have their usefulness and their worth. But what if you could transform your "lead-like" real estate investments into solid gold? What if you could locate and purchase a property and then through subjecting that investment to powerful potions and fantastical formulas be left with a hunk of 24K magic in your hand? Better still, like the alchemists of old, what if you could do it more quickly?

Think of me as a modern-day alchemist – and you as my trusty assistant – who through using the proper formulas can convert everyday real estate investments into gold-generating machines.

How Will We Do That?

We must first begin with sourcing the proper material, or lead if you want to continue with the analogy, and that, dear readers, is apartments. Other alchemists may swear by single-family homes, commercial office buildings or even mobile home parks, but my formulas work most powerfully, quickly and profitably with small apartment buildings (defined as five to 100 units).

Through this book, we'll descend into my laboratory and begin the transformational process, using two recent investments of mine as the base metals. One is surely lead (a real challenge with a 22% occupancy), the other at 91% occupancy more like shiny silver, but both ready to reach gold status.

You'll walk beside me every step of the way, fully learning each formula, until you can practice your own alchemical processes.

Turn the page and join me on this journey – cone-shaped hat, optional.

Chapter 2
The Base Metals

"Money is only a tool. It will take you wherever you wish, but it will not replace you as the driver."

– Ayn Rand

Step into my laboratory, trusty assistant, and take a look at the raw materials on which we will work our magic. The "base metals" selected for this exercise (the lead and silver mentioned in the Introduction) are two actual deals of mine. What that means is none of this is theoretical with pie-in-the-sky numbers and wishful thinking. Two real deals done (or being done) by me.

Before we begin, let me tell you a bit about how I "source" my base metals (aka deals). If you are picturing me in a miner's helmet and carrying a pickaxe, you couldn't be further from the truth. I don't "mine" many of my deals. I have partners (members of my own Wealth Mastermind Network™) who do that for me and earn a chunk of change from doing so. (That's why THEY need the pickaxes!)

Bonus Resource

The Wealth Mastermind Network (WMN) member and coaching client who found my "shiny silver" deal worked with her coach and my proprietary Greenlight Software™ to analyze its potential.

When they got the "green light," they passed it to me, I contacted the broker and the rest is history. For her part in the transaction, the WMN member received a $25,000 check at closing. Learn more about the Wealth Mastermind Network and the Greenlight Software in Chapter 7 Summary of Resources and Offers.

Before I created my trusty WMN, however, I generally scouted deals on my own. My first was a fourplex that I purchased in 2003. A second (identical) fourplex just down the road followed soon thereafter. At that point, I owned eight doors.

As I raised my profile among buyers and sellers in the area, people started marketing to me. A local wholesaler, Howard, brought me my next deal – a 10-unit property. Howard posted a flyer at our Saturday real estate club meeting. Do you know what my first thought was when I saw that flyer? "Gee, Lance, are you ready for 10 units?"

The human mind is a funny thing. At that point, I already owned eight doors, but my old belief systems still nagged me about whether I could handle 10 more. Gimme a break! Fortunately, I had started my mindset training and recognized the source of the noise. I was able to silence it long enough to call the number on the flyer.

What About Howard?

Howard was a successful single-family wholesaler and he was flipping the 10-unit for $150,000 ($15,000 per door – the good old days!). However, he didn't have the property under contract. He thought that apartments were different than houses and he wanted to learn about small apartments to quickly scale his cash flow. Long story short: He arranged a meeting between me and the mom-and-pop owner. I got the property under contract and paid Howard a very healthy $10,000 finder's fee. (Howard later attended my very first seminar in 2007.)

You could say that the seeds of what would be my WMN were planted all the way back then. And, what worked then works just as well now. When it comes to sourcing your "base metals" you could do worse than partnering with active, single-family wholesalers like Howard.

How Do You Find Wholesalers?

Simple. Join your local real estate club(s) and start asking, "Who are the active wholesalers?" It may take some time and a few phone calls, but sooner or later you'll get a fairly healthy list that may extend beyond your region and into the nation.

Once you have a list, approach the active wholesalers in whatever market(s) you're interested in and proposition them. (No, I don't mean like that!) Tell them you'll pay finder's fees for every small apartment deal they bring you. Most will do it just for the exposure because they lack what you have – small apartments knowledge and access to a network of established connections.

Besides the potential knowledge-transfer benefit, offer and pay them generous finder fees. And only invest your precious time and energy with active wholesalers – the 5% who are doing the deals in that market.

Once you find a few interested parties, here's how you keep them motivated:

1. Give them very specific criteria on what you want (and don't want). You don't want them feeling they are wasting their time (or yours). Make it fifth grade simple.
2. Be very responsive when they send you a lead. Either jump on making an offer or quickly explain how it doesn't fit what you're looking for. Delay kills deals.
3. Consider paying advances against finder fees for signed letters of intent (LOIs) and contracts. Get them into the money early. (I currently rebate my Small Apartments School tuition with the first three greenlight leads, whether I buy one or not. I'm demonstrating I'm serious).

Today, after 20-some years in the business, I have a huge network, not only of scouts, but of lenders, rehabbers, management companies and more.

Speaking of lenders, if you, like most real estate investors, spend an inordinate amount of time fretting over the "raising money" part of the deal, I can help. My Special Report, How to Raise Private

Money, lays out my four-part formula for raising any amount of money for any type of real estate. Two first-timers used this formula and system to purchase small apartments valued at $6 million in just 10 months, using none of their own cash or credit.

Bonus Resource
Special Report: How to Raise Private Money
www.AptAlchemyBook.com/RPM

Turning Lead Into Gold

My WMN members are partners in the alchemical process and sometimes, together, we transform lead into gold. That's what happened with my 44-unit West Virginia project. When we discovered it, the occupancy rate struggled along at about 22%. (I couldn't have been happier to find something with such a huge potential upside.)

Other times, WMN members locate a piece of shiny silver, like the 56-unit Oklahoma property that had a fairly impressive 91% occupancy. Can we do better? I think we can with the Apartment Alchemy I plan to show you.

I share this because I don't want you to discount any potential apartment deal without running the "fantastical formulas." Yes, you can make big money from fixing poorly run apartments – the ones with low occupancy and below-market rents. (My friend, Ron LeGrand, calls them UGLY properties or, more to the point, "making chicken salad out of chicken you-know-what.")

However, you can have just as much upside with PRETTY properties. If you are neglecting opportunities when you see occupancy rates of 90% or above, you're ignoring big profit potential. Pretty properties can get prettier. You don't always have to deal with junkers. That's what I call turning silver into gold.

Let's begin our alchemical analysis with the Oklahoma property.

Ridgewood Village Apartments, Moore, Oklahoma (part of the Oklahoma City metropolitan area)

- 56 units as well as a small commercial building, which houses a dog grooming, boarding and training business
- 91% occupancy
- The property is two blocks from a Starbucks and sits on a frontage road, facing I-35. On the backside, it's surrounded by a residential neighborhood. A nice elementary school is three minutes walking distance from the property and nestled amongst the homes.

"How do you improve that?" you may be wondering. Glad you asked. Because I'm going to show you how I intend to create $1.5 million in value in fairly short order. But first, let's continue our examination of the Oklahoma opportunity.

Finding the upside in a situation that already appears to be pretty rosy can often be summed up in two very powerful words – lazy management.

How I Learned To LOVE Lazy Management

Well, let me clarify. We love lazy management on the part of the seller's management, not with us! Suboptimal management can typically be found with small mom-and-pop-type, self-managed apartments. I'm not throwing shade at mom-and-pop places. Some of my best deals have come from them and many have become valued members of the WMN and great partners in my deals.

The biggest strike against self-managed, mom-and-poppers is they operate their properties more as a hobby than as a business. After all, their small apartments are typically not their main source of cash flow. But those apartments can be the source of their greatest aggravation and a strain on their already limited and precious time. They naturally devote the bulk of their time to whatever other activity produces their main cash flow. And, they avoid "rocking the boat" with their residents for fear of the aggravation of losing one and having to invest the time (and money) to replace them.

For example, mom and pop rarely raise rent. ("We wouldn't dare raise Mildred's $395 rent. She's been with us for years and we might lose her.")

Mom and pop also rarely institute and collect "other income" policies like pet fees, late fees, utility fees and WiFi fees. Why? Again, the concern of losing someone and having to replace them. If small apartments are your "hobby" or "side business," they get the least amount of attention. It's natural. Often, the are undercapitalized to make the improvements that can yield 40+% annual ROI or even basic repairs. This can lead to deferred maintenance and a hit on the property's marketability.

Finally, as part-time operators, mom and pop typically don't work on reducing the two biggest expenses they have: property taxes and insurance. They generally don't shop their insurance bill because their agent, Joe, is their best friend's cousin and a good guy. ("I'm sure Joe is taking good care of us.") They would never think to dispute their property taxes with the county; that's another time sink for them. (Actually, it's zero work when you hire it out on a contingency basis.)

That's why small apartments are so attractive. Mom-and-pop apartments represent low-hanging fruit. (One caveat: WMN members who happen to be mom-and-pop operators don't fit that mold. They studied the alchemical formulas with yours truly and turned lead, brass, copper or silver into pure gold – using other people's time, talent and money!)

What may surprise you, however, is that lazy management also can be found among professional management companies, which brings me back to the Oklahoma property. This 56-unit, 91% occupancy gem was stagnating under lazy management.

How lazy were they? I'm glad you asked.

The property management company was so lazy, they refused to come to the property to provide access to the units during my due diligence inspections. They wouldn't even give us access to the keys. The seller's broker (a charming and most obliging lady) had to drive from Dallas to Oklahoma City to meet me and my management team with the keys. Then she drove back to Dallas.

For the next two days, we walked the units ourselves, unsupervised. That's lazy management! Careful property managers escort potential buyers every minute of their visit. They control which units you see (usually the best of the best) and monitor any conversation you may have with residents or vendors.

During those two days, we had free rein. We walked and sized up each unit and talked with several residents. In speaking with residents, we heard complaint after complaint, "They never fix anything. I've been calling for weeks. There's no one on site. The neighbors play their music loud. They don't care. I'm leaving."

But I knew this even before I went under contract. How?

I "mystery shopped" the property and the competition. In other words, I collected intel.

Lance Edwards, International Spy

The first time I saw Ridgewood was on a Friday at 5 p.m. I was in town doing due diligence on another property I had under contract (and ended up abandoning – I'll save that story for another book). I walked onto the grounds at Ridgewood and asked the first couple I saw sitting outside their apartment, "Can you tell me where the leasing office is?"

You know how they talk about hitting an artery and getting a "gusher?" Well, I hit a couple of gushers in these two. They immediately opened up (and frankly wouldn't shut up), warning me off. "You don't want to live here. The management is lazy. There's no one on site. They don't fix anything. A man like you and at your age, you don't want to live here." (I never quite figured out what they meant by my age. Hmmm.)

Finally, I asked the $64,000 question (actually it turned out to be the $1.5 million question). "Well then, why don't you just move?"

Their answer had the stirring sound of cash registers ringing in my ears.

"Because everywhere else is more expensive." Cha-ching.

Thanks to those two gushers, I knew the alchemical potion to pour on this property:

Serve the residents. Charge service fees in exchange for value. Elevate the property to market rents. Eliminate wasteful expenses along the way.

This is the same thing any smart business does, and this is your strategy whether you are converting lead to gold, or silver to gold, through apartment alchemy.

Finally, since it was already evening, I drove the residential neighborhood, waiting for nightfall, then camped in the parking lot to see what happened at night. Were there droves of marauding hoodlums and gangsters? Were residents tossing empty beer cans out their front door? Street walkers working the corner?

Nope. Nothing. Quiet. Just people coming home from work. However, in the shadow of lazy management, I counted a number of inoperable security lights. And, for the first time, I noticed each apartment door had an entry lamp, but many were not lit and most were hanging loose. (That's a screwdriver repair.) I was discovering more and more low-hanging fruit.

Armed with this information, the next step was to evaluate how big the opportunity was. The next morning, I expanded my mystery shopping (my research). I visited the nearest competitor 0.3 miles away. This was a 48-unit property but, unlike Ridgewood, it had an on-site leasing agent for walk-up traffic like me.

The property was professionally managed, clean and tidy, and obviously tended to (unlike Ridgewood which had apartment doors with mismatched paint and at least two of them installed upside down).

A pleasant young woman greeted me and I used my standard mystery shopping script (it works on the phone or in person), "Hi, my name is Lance. I'm looking for an apartment to rent. I'm not exactly sure what size so can you show me a one-bedroom and a two-bedroom?" She told me she only had two vacancies (96% occupancy) and she had one of each.

She gave me the tour and I peppered her with questions.

Q: What are the rents?
A: $745 for the one bedroom and $945 for the two bedroom.

Q: How big are the units?
A: The one bedroom is 700 square feet and the two bedroom is 900 square feet.

Q: Is there a move-in special?
A: Yes, $299 with good credit.

Q: Is there an on-site maintenance person?
A: Yes. (I bumped into him after my tour. His name's Gerald and he's worked there seven years. Maintenance requests are made via a phone app.)

Q: Are there other fees?
A: Yes, a partial billback for water.

The units she showed me had received upgrades to match what we WMN members call our "Decorator Unit" style: luxury vinyl laminate flooring throughout (which looks like wood), resurfaced kitchen and bath countertops, updated brush nickel light fixtures, and new kitchen cabinet doors and hardware on the existing cabinets.

Unfortunately, they had retained the old standard white walls and beat-up 40-year-old baseboards with 40 coats of white paint covering 1,000 dings and dents. Nothing super fancy but at least not your standard brown carpet and white-walled apartment. The one "luxury item" for this Class B-/C unit was the dishwasher.

She completed my tour, and I followed her back to the office. I was keen to hear her "close." I sat in the chair and anxiously awaited her to sign me up.

Crickets. Nothing. Nada.

The close was nonexistent. She didn't stick an application under my nose. She didn't collect a shred of information on me. She didn't ask me what I thought or when I might want to move. She just sat there. Leasing rock star she was not. Having concluded my assessment, I thanked her and left.

Later on, I thought maybe I caught the leasing agent on a bad day, so I invited my management company to do their own mystery shop of the same complex. Results: Identical.

I had identified another ingredient in my power potion: Add superior marketing (which is the real weapon of any business).

More on that later.

Excited over the project, I rushed back to my hotel to submit an offer and get this property tied down. There was more evaluation to be done but that wasn't going to happen until I got it under contract and into due diligence.

For example, I still had no idea of the condition of Ridgewood's interior units and how much rehab might be needed for the updates. I entered a BIG rehab estimate into my Greenlight Software, and it still came up "Greenlight" at the Ask Price.

Where's The Green Light?

I should probably stop here and describe the Greenlight Software because it's one of the tools I use to act quickly and with confidence.

The main fear that newbies have in making offers on apartments is the fear of overpaying. As a result, two bad things happen: 1) they make no offers or 2) they offer too little – both with the same result, no offers are accepted, and no deals get done.

To address that fear among my training clients, I created my Greenlight Software. Greenlight Software makes the sophisticated process of deal analysis and offer making "fifth grade simple." (I was inspired to do this when a fifth grader attended my training with his Dad and bought a duplex 90 days later – with Dad's help).

Simply enter the basic information about an apartment complex (number of units, rents, occupancy, expenses, market information). Then "flip the switch," so to speak, and the Greenlight Software performs rigorous calculations behind the curtain to give a redlight/greenlight indicator. (I call it fifth grade simple, but didn't we learn colors in kindergarten?) Greenlight means do it. Redlight means not yet or not without some adjustment. Think of the full-priced offers you can make in confidence.

Once I got the greenlight, off went our standard LOI to the broker. My offer was quickly accepted, and the next step was the contract. I prepared the contract using the standard state form for Oklahoma, which the broker provided me.

My signed LOI gave me the standard 45 days of due diligence and 60 days to close, plus an extra 30 days (if needed) for financing.

However, I was dependent on the lazy management company to feed me all the financial due diligence information (leases, service agreements, rent rolls, income and expense statements, etc.). I'd already seen their sense of urgency (or lack thereof) and wasn't willing to be on the clock waiting for those lazy souls. So I added my secret weapon…

The "I Won't Be Penalized By Your Laziness" Clause

Rather than just explain it, here's the actual language I added to the Addendum Page of the contract:

> 5) Within three business days from Time Reference Date (*DD Delivery Period*), Seller shall deliver to Buyer the due diligence information specified in Exhibit A (DD Info). In the event some of the DD Info is not in Seller's possession, Seller shall reply so in writing to Buyer. If any single item identified in Exhibit A is not fully delivered, or in the alternative, Seller has not responded in writing that such information does not exist or is not available, during the DD Delivery Period, the Time Reference Date shall be extended by such time that the DD Info has not been fully delivered or responded to.

This saved me.

I signed the contract on December 4. Would you like to guess how long it took them to fully deliver the information to me? Come on. Take a guess. Seven days? Two weeks? Three weeks? If you said one month, congratulations! You win a chicken dinner.

My contract timeline started on January 4 – exactly one month after the contract was signed. Now, without that language, I would have had to renegotiate for more time due to lack of basic information.

This clause alone is worth the price of this book, so be sure to use it! Feel free to customize this language in your own contracts. A few points to note:

1. You can substitute "Effective Date" for "Time Reference Date." (Time Reference Date is a term unique to Oklahoma contracts.)
2. If your contract doesn't have a blank Addendum Page (and most don't), just create one in Word and type away to your heart's delight. Label it "Addendum 1" on the header and write "See Addendum 1" somewhere in the body of your contract.
3. Of course, just as I teach, have an attorney review and bless the final form before transmittal. If you don't have an attorney, you can get one inexpensively at LegalShield.com (I think it's $39/month) and they'll review contracts. For my own coaching clients, I offer a comprehensive review before legal blessing.

This clause worked so well that the seller couldn't believe his management company's laziness cost him a month when he learned about it. He even paid an attorney to tell him what the contract said about the timeline! Wow. It's obvious. Maybe you should have paid an attorney (like I recommend) before you signed the contract. Maybe you should have been paying more attention to your own transaction. Anyway, thanks to my clause, it's not my problem.

Finally, I'm under contract. That's the first critical milestone in the alchemical process. Normally I teach Network members to collect all pertinent financial information and complete financial due diligence before committing to physical due diligence, but I didn't follow my own rules. Here's why…

It was early December, and I didn't want to lose momentum due to the holidays. (Remember, this deal had a prospective $1.5 million in value. Would you wait?) So, I bit the bullet and scheduled the on-site inspections with my management company for December 15 and 16, less than two weeks after signing the contract. The management company performed the most comprehensive due diligence that I've ever seen done (outside of myself).

When my Operations Director and I arrived on site the morning of the 15th, the management company's due diligence TEAM was already there. I counted five people. They had arrived en masse.

The "TEAM"

- Aaron, the inspector
- Two ladies who audited every lease and application at the management company's office
- The in-house HVAC man to check out that equipment
- A roof contractor to inspect the roofs
- Later the plumber showed up to "scope" the lines (run a camera down the main lines searching for breaks or obstructions – there were none).

Truth Is Stranger Than Fiction

If you've never walked apartment units, let me warn you...

You never know what you'll see on due diligence inspections.

Have you heard the saying, "I can't believe how some people live?" Well, let me testify, it's true.

Here's a sampling of what I saw on this tour: a hoarder's unit, a bare-bones bed-and-TV-only unit, a trash dump disguised as an apartment, a pet iguana, a pot plant (I discovered pot is legal in Oklahoma), and a rottweiler (in a cage). Apparently the rottweiler was only in the cage when the resident was out. How can I know that?

Because the dog's droppings were scattered across the entire floor of that apartment, covering the unit. Disgusting. Yet another exhibit to hold up as testament to the laziness of the management company. They obviously never performed periodic inspections. Can you guess which resident is getting the boot for health violations as soon as I take over?

But what I discovered was surprisingly better than expected. Recall my competitor with the luxury vinyl laminate floors? Good news! Over 50% of the units at Ridgewood had already been upgraded to luxury vinyl laminate (with no rent increase). Cha-ching. More low-hanging fruit which I'll quantify in just a moment.

Back To More Profitable Discoveries

Would you believe 67% of the residents were pet owners of at least one pet but only 20% of the residents were being charged the $20 per month pet rent per pet? Cha-ching again.

Now, you might be thinking, "Lance, how big a difference can $20 per month per unit make?" Hold that thought. In the next chapter, we'll cover the fantastical formulas (aka the Laws of Apartment Alchemy) and you'll see how that one small operational change is worth $97,000 to me and my investors.

By the end of the first day, between me and my management team companion, Aaron, the full plan was taking shape. It was as I had imagined from my first unofficial drop-by on that sole Friday evening, except better. There was so much low-hanging fruit I was even more excited. But at the restaurant that evening, alone over my chicken fajitas, I had my epiphany.

It's that old real estate truism: location, location, location.

I had spent a whole day of exposure to just how lazy this management company was. Resident after resident had the same story. It was evidenced in the deferred maintenance. However, the property consistently runs above 90% occupancy DESPITE lazy management.

How could such a poorly run business be this successful in spite of itself? That's the question I asked over and over until it finally hit me, while I was reaching for the salsa...

It's the location on I-35 where -- I don't know -- tens of thousands of cars drive by every day. That's FREE advertising for which billboard advertisers pay $2,500 per month. This property has massive FREE advertising.

Ever seen those signs at apartments when you're stuck in traffic after a long hard day? "If You Lived Here, You'd Be Home Now." With my own sign and an on-site leasing presence, plus a little curb appeal improvement, we could be pushing 100% occupancy (with a waiting list).

I couldn't sleep that night rolling the possibilities over in my head.

The next morning, I met the Regional Manager from the

management company, Zeta. Zeta is Property Management Queen over Central Oklahoma and comes widely recommended from my reference checks so I used the opportunity to pick her brain, "Zeta, how would you approach this property?"

Her answer, "This property's a money maker. We're going to put someone on site, improve the service, collect "other income" and bump the rents to market rate with every renewal (as-is). On the move-outs, we'll update the units for a second rent bump to not just match the competitor but beat them."

Bingo. She just validated my basic strategy. At this point, I'm less than two weeks into this project and I already know there's no turning back.

Bonus: Here's the Due Diligence Inspection Report Scope of Items that I use. I ask my inspectors to deliver a full accounting of the property's condition in writing and this is exactly what they use.

Units

1. Unit #
2. # BR / # BA?
3. Occupied?
4. Ask resident, "Are you having any problems?"

Air And Water

1. Water temperature – hot and cold
2. Toilet / sinks / shower / tub draining properly
3. Toilet / sinks / shower / tub leaks
4. Air temperature from HVAC
5. Electrical outlets work

Components

1. Kitchen cabinet condition
2. Kitchen countertop type / condition
3. Tub and/or shower condition
4. Windows condition

5. Ceiling fan condition / works
6. Appliances work / condition / colors
7. Ceiling stains from leaks?
8. Flooring type / condition

Pets

1. # pets / what type (dogs: small or large)

Equipment

1. Copper or aluminum wiring / breakers or fuses / Federal Pacific?
2. Boiler / Hot Water Heaters
3. HVAC equipment type / condition / operation
4. Equipment room condition
5. Internet
6. Cable TV
7. Emergency equipment and exit signs / fire extinguishers at code
8. Emergency stairs at code
9. Laundromat area and equipment

Other

1. Roof condition
2. Foundation condition
3. Scope sewer lines
4. Termite / bed bug / pest inspection
5. Presence of asbestos or lead

Bonus Resources Summary

Wealth Mastermind Network (WMN) and Greenlight Software Summary, Chapter 7

Special Report: How to Raise Private Money
www.AptAlchemyBook.com/RPM

Chapter 3
Fantastical Formulas

"You will never reach your true potential living life in comfort and routine. You've got to take some risks."

–Kylie Francis

Over the centuries, alchemists failed to secure the recipe for creating gold. Why? Personally, I believe they were overcomplicating it (like most people do). Why do I say that? Because the greatest foundational breakthroughs in understanding the universe are remarkably simple recipes. For example...

Newton's First Law of Motion: $F = M * A$
Einstein's Theory of Relativity: $E = M * C2$

A fifth grader can understand the math. Well, the ultimate formula in Apartment Alchemy is also incredibly simple:

First Law of Apartment Alchemy:
Value = NOI / Market Cap Rate

Second Law of Apartment Alchemy:
NOI = Revenue - Expenses
(NOI means Net Operating Income.)

That's it. Memorize these formulas or tattoo them on your arm.

Don't underestimate the power of the formulas just because the math is fifth grade simple. The magic is in their application. Did you know NASA used Newton's simple First Law of Motion formula to land a man on the moon, 239,000 miles away? That's quite an achievement from something defined nearly 300 years prior – 1686 to be exact.

You can achieve something pretty spectacular yourself by applying the First and Second Laws of Apartment Alchemy, transforming any base metal into gold.

Applying The Laws

So, let's apply the First and Second Laws to my Oklahoma project and get your creative alchemist juices flowing in your own business. My first job upon returning home to Florida after the inspections was to quantify the returns of my low-hanging fruit discoveries and quantify the amount of energy (time and capital) needed to optimize the returns (i.e. maximize the ROI). Let's apply the laws.

First Law of Apartment Alchemy:
Value = NOI / Market Cap Rate

Second Law of Apartment Alchemy:
NOI = Revenue - Expenses

Note: WMN members have the Greenlight Software to perform these calculations for them. However, I'm old school (I learned math before calculators existed), so I'm going to demonstrate how fifth grade simple it is to exactly compute how much each property tweak is worth to you. You don't need a calculator; you just need the back of an envelope and a pencil. Let's apply this fantastical formula to the Oklahoma property in a test case I like to call:

Apartment Alchemy Formula #1: The Cost Of Not Raising Mildred's Rent ($930,000 Value Capturing Just Half Of The Rent Gap)

Let's return to our typical mom-and-pop operator who doesn't dare raise the rent on Mildred because she's been with them forever. What's that decision costing them? And when you buy their property, what's it worth to you to raise the rents to market?

Here's the market rent analysis provided in the Offering Memorandum (OM) of Ridgewood and validated by me:

Unit Type	Ridgewood today (rent per sq. ft.)	0.3 Mile competitor (rent per sq. ft.)
1 BR	$0.76	$1.00
2 BR	$0.81	$0.92

As you can see, Ridgewood's rent is way below market.

In fact, the rents for the competitor have gone up since the OM was done. Recall my mystery shopping results from the former chapter: $745 rent for a 700 square foot one-bedroom is $1.06 versus $1.00, but let's stay conservative and stick with $1.00.

Notice the one bedroom rent at the competitor is 33% higher than Ridgewood ($1.00/$0.76). The rent gap is biggest in one bedrooms, which is great news, because Ridgewood is largely one-bedrooms (86% one bedroom; 14% two bedroom).

We'll remain conservative and assume we only capture half of that increase, or a 16% rent increase at Ridgewood. One bedrooms are $600 so a $16% rent increase is basically $100. Let's assume $100 rent increase across the board. Now here comes the alchemy...

The Second Law says NOI = Revenue - Expenses, so revenue increases with rent hikes.

Do the expenses increase when we raise rent? Uh... NO. The expense increase is ZERO. This is the alchemy in incremental improvements – they drop to the bottom line, to NOI.

So how much did the value increase? Time to consider the First Law of Apartment Alchemy. Assuming the average occupancy is

90% due to move-outs, etc., let's initially look at the value increase from raising the rent $100 on just one unit, where the market cap rate is 6.5%.

$$\text{Value} = \text{NOI} / \text{Market Cap Rate}$$
$$\text{Value Increase} = \$100 * 12 \text{ mos} * 90\% / 6.5\% = \$16{,}615 \text{ per unit!}$$

So for every mom-and-pop operator who doesn't raise the rent, it's costing them $16,600 for every $100 rent increase, or $1,660 for every $10 rent increase per door!

Ridgewood has 56 doors so the opportunity in bumping the rents $100 is:

$$\$16{,}600 \text{ per door} * 56 \text{ doors} = \$930{,}000!$$

Cha-ching. (You might want to start counting the cha-chings!) That's $930,000 to me and my investors from being a better operator.

Most, if not all, can be captured without much CapEx (capital expenditures). We just need to serve the residents. Remember, they already know their rent is low. (They told me so.)

I don't intend to go in day one and increase everyone's rents. First of all, I can't legally; they have leases. However, we can do it with the new rentals. And we can do it on the renewals (after we demonstrate that we're providing better service). That's why our approach is a "two-step" process...

Service First, Upgrade Second

Step 1: Service. Demonstrate professional service with on-site management immediately upon take-over. Increase the revenue (rent bump #1 and other income increases) with little to no CapEx.

Step 2: Upgrade. With each move-out, invest CapEx and update the unit interiors for a second rent bump with each new resident.

Are you getting the idea? Excited? I hope so. We're just getting started.

Apartment Alchemy Formula #2: The Cost Of Not Collecting Other Income ($97,000 Value Collecting Pet Fees)

Can you guess the number one amenity to renters? Accepting pets. 67% of U.S. households own at least one pet, but less than 40% of apartments accept pets. An even smaller percentage actually cater to pet owners as pet friendly. That's what I call a supply and demand imbalance. Cha-ching.

As you can see, pet-friendly properties are tough to find. As a result of the scarcity, pet owners are ready, willing and able to pay extra rent and non-refundable pet deposits just to have a place for little Fluffy. Fortunately, this property is already pet friendly. (If it wasn't, I'd switch it because of what I'm about to demonstrate, just as I'm doing with my West Virginia property.)

It's A Dog's Life

This is probably the perfect place to stop for a moment and illustrate how attached people are to their pets, starring none other than yours truly and his lovely wife, Kim. (I'll keep this brief because the long version is a real tear jerker.)

About five years ago while taking our typical Saturday morning walk in Houston, a little mini yellow lab-looking dog followed Kim and I home.

The poor little guy wasn't much to look at. His bones were showing. He had a "24-Hour Fitness" lanyard tied around his neck as a collar. If you touched his breastbone, you could feel a metal BB where he had been shot. We took him to the vet who told us he had heartworms and was severely malnourished. This little pup had had a rough life.

Kim posted "Dog Found" ads online and with the gate sentry. No one claimed him, but one nice couple offered to take him if no one else would. Kim asked if we could keep him and I refused. We had just signed a contract on our beach house in Florida and I didn't want to be traveling back and forth with a dog. Kim sadly saw the logic and agreed with me.

The nice couple came by on Sunday morning and spent two hours with the little guy in our backyard. The woman finally said, "We'll take him," and off they drove with the dog. Kim was in tears and, frankly, I felt sad too.

Three hours later, the woman called back and said her husband changed his mind and she needed to return the dog. Kim was ecstatic. As they pulled into our driveway and with the car still moving, the little guy leaped out of the passenger side window, ran to me and jumped up into my arms. And that was that. He's been with us ever since.

Kim immediately doted on him and when she asked, "What shall we call him?" My response was immediate, "Riley. It's clear he's going to live the Life of Riley."

From Slumdog To Millionaire

Riley picked well that weekend. In the blink of an eye he went from slumdog to millionaire.

Riley became Kim's "baby doggy." And that's when my understanding of the pet industry began. Riley lives better than me, eats better than me and sleeps better than me.

When I accompany Kim to the vet's office, I see a business that is packed. Pet owners spend LOTS of money on their furry family members.

Three years ago, I told Kim, "One day we're going into the pet business, catering to well-to-do owners." I didn't think of it until the "pet-friendly" Ridgewood project crossed my desk.

West Virginia became my pet-friendly test case. We had been turning down pet owners with a No Pets Policy. Right after lifting that policy, the next three leases were pet owners who paid the extra rent and fees and never batted an eye. We're standardizing on pet-friendly going forward!

At Ridgewood, we have two dog grooming and boarding businesses on either end of the property. I'm the landlord for one as she runs her business in my building. I envision an alliance with at least one of those businesses where I can advertise: "On-site pet grooming, dog-walking, pet hotel, dog park, doggy day care, pet parties..." We'll advertise our pet-friendly properties with the "Life of Riley Seal of Approval." He'll be famous. I'm naming the dog parks and buildings after my investors and students who make it possible.

Since we walked every unit in Oklahoma, we knew the pet situation at Ridgewood. A whopping 67% of residents own at least one pet and each lease states requires a $350 non-refundable pet deposit and $20 extra rent per month per pet.

However, you remember our lazy management company? The lazy management company only collects pet fees on 20% of the units! They're not collecting on 47% of the units which are known to have pets. So, let's get the cauldron out and perform a little alchemy on pet fees. How much value is created by simply collecting the $20 per month per pet (we'll assume only one pet per unit which is quite conservative). But I am counting the pet iguana I saw in the inspections! Back to the First Law:

$$\text{Value} = \text{NOI} / \text{Market Cap Rate}$$
$$\text{Value} = \$20 * 12 \text{ months} * 47\% * 56 \text{ units} / 6.5\% = \$97,000!$$

Add $97,000 to the tally. We're now at $1,027,000 of alchemical value gain. But here's an even BIGGER idea...

Apartment Alchemy Formula #3: The Cost Of Poor Marketing ($254,000 Value Adding Superior Marketing)

You may recall that I mentioned superior marketing would be a key aspect of my strategy. So, let's build on this high-demand "pet-friendly" model which Ridgewood already serves.

Remember, occupancy is currently 91% with lazy management, zero marketing, and no on-site presence to show and lease units.

I ask, "Why not 100% occupancy with a waiting list?" (I always like to ask challenging and empowering questions.)

How about we combine the property's I-35 frontage presence

(and its incredible FREE drive-by traffic) with the property's existing "pet-friendly" theme (the number one amenity sought by renters)?

So, here's the sign (I'm thinking maybe a billboard) I want to install in the first 90 days facing interstate highway I-35:

```
NEW On-site Management! If You Lived Here,
You'd Be Home Now! Pet-Friendly! Call 555-1212
                   or Stop By
```

What's that sign worth to me and my investors if I increase occupancy just 4% from 91% to 95% at the current rents, assuming no rent increase? Again, I'm always conservative in my projections. My management company thinks I'm overly conservative but hey, this is my money and my investors' money going into these projects.

Let's look at it through the lens of the First Law.

$$\text{Value} = \text{NOI} / \text{Market Cap Rate}$$
$$\text{Value} = \$615 \text{ avg rent} * 12 \text{ mos} * 4\% * 56 \text{ units} / 6.5\% = \$254,000$$

Add $254,000 to the tally. We're now at $1,281,000 gold value gain to me and my investors. But let's look at one more powerful alchemical formula.

Apartment Alchemy Formula #4: The Cost Of Not Charging Other Income ($124,000 Collecting WiFi Fees)

An existing provision in the leases is that the residents pay $20 per month for property-provided Internet. At this point, I bet you can guess what kind of job the lazy management company is doing in collecting that $20 the owner is entitled to.

Only 30% are billed the $20! When you think about the WiFi fees

Fantastical Formulas

and the pet fees are simply a matter of enforcing the leases. By now, you understand the fifth grade math, assuming 90% occupancy.

$$\text{Value} = \text{NOI} / \text{Market Cap Rate}$$
$$\text{Value} = \$20 * 12 \text{ mos} * (90\%-30\%) * 56 \text{ units} / 6.5\% = \$124,000$$

Our grand total (for now) in value gain from apartment alchemy is $1,405,000 captured with little to no CapEx! Before we finish this discussion, I'll show you one final application of apartment alchemy, except this time we focus on the "expense side" of the Second Law.

Apartment Alchemy Formula #5: The Cost Of Wasteful Expenses ($166,000 Cutting Water Leaks)

Here's something I discovered back home when I finally received the property's finances and bills. The water bill in Building A is double the water bill in Building B (and the buildings are mirror images of each other). Building A has an average monthly bill of $900; Building B's is $1,800!

How is that possible? Water leaks. There's $900 per month going down the sewer. Literally! Actually, my inspector friend, Aaron, identified a number of leaks in his report. But you never realize how much water leaks really cost you in an apartment.

Again, the lazy management company never caught this. You would think that the person writing the checks would have said, "Hey, has anyone noticed that the water bill is double on Building B?" But nope. They blindly wrote away the owner's cash flow.

Taking into account the $10,800 per year running down the sewer, you as an Apartment Alchemist can now compute the impact on the value when we stop the leaks and my management team implements a water conservation program (again at very little CapEx).

$$\text{Value} = \text{NOI} / \text{Market Cap Rate}$$
$$\text{Value} = \$900 * 12 \text{ months} / 6.5\% = \$166,000.$$

What's the tally now, Johnny? Drum roll, please.

Five fantastical formulas based on the First and Second Laws of Apartment Alchemy captured a whopping $1,571,000 for me and my investors on one project with very little CapEx! All this came from operating better, offering real service and marketing smart.

How Many Projects Like This Do You Need?

Would you believe $1,571,000 is not the real grand total? Another $900,000 can be realized from pushing the rents to market, investing CapEx and updating interiors on the move-outs. In fact, the game never ends. That's the fun part – at least for me. But you get the point. This is the alchemy that gets me excited, and I hope it's done the same for you.

Remember, these figures aren't "funny money." I've validated my projections through my own due diligence and that of my management company (which manages 2,000 doors in Central Oklahoma and 20,000 doors nationally). Most importantly, I didn't try to fly solo; I leveraged my team. Apartment alchemy can be dangerous when performed alone. If attempted without expert assistance, rather than gold, you might accidentally create radioactive uranium.

The Value Of A Team

The value of a team is probably the single most important lesson I have learned on my 20-year real estate investing journey. I preach this at every bootcamp I teach. This is NOT a solopreneur activity.

This isn't something I discovered on my own. Many have written about it. Jim Collins in his classic book, "Good to Great," talks about having "the right people on the bus," meaning the right team. Verne Harnish in his bestseller, "Scaling Up," defines the four components of growth as people, strategy, execution and cash. It might surprise you to learn that "people" is always the most limiting element.

My mentor, Dan Sullivan, recently released a book with

Benjamin Hardy which focuses exclusively on the people issue. It's called "Who Not How." This book theme is at the core of all entrepreneurship. Too many aspiring entrepreneurs ask, "How do I do something?" The "how" question simply defines a job for yourself – with a tyrant for a boss (you).

The more powerful question posed by Dan Sullivan that we should always ask ourselves is: "Who can do it for me?" Dan and Benjamin write, "When you're trying to accomplish something challenging or difficult that you've never done before, you probably need a Who. Let me say that another way: You absolutely need a Who if you're trying to accomplish something new and challenging, unless you're fine not getting the result you want in the near future."

And frankly, that's the number one reason most aspiring real estate entrepreneurs struggle – they don't have a trusted "who" infrastructure in place to leverage while trying to accomplish something challenging – like starting their own business in small apartments.

My WMN is the perfect example of the power of a team and connecting with all sorts of smart "whos." Being a part of the network means you get the great education, the "hows," but you also get the "whos" in the form of the people I trust with my own deals. The WMN team consists of lenders, management companies, insurers, buyers and other trusted advisors you need for success – all "greenlighted" and done for you.

Before we close out this chapter, let me walk you through the closing on the Ridgewood Apartment, as well as a duplex I own in Toledo. (Consider it a bonus.)

The Ridgewood closing gave me the opportunity to practice an important skill – one that's needed in every deal and taught on the final day of my bootcamps. It's called "Managing the Anxiety Curve."

In a brokered transaction, there are three players: the Agent (representing the Seller), the Seller and the Buyer (in this case, me). Now imagine that there was a device which we could permanently strap to the arm of a human being and instantaneously measure their anxiety level.

Then imagine that over the timeline of a transaction – from contracting to closing – we could chart the anxiety level of each player. What we would observe is the "Anxiety Curves" of each player, sketched in the diagram below.

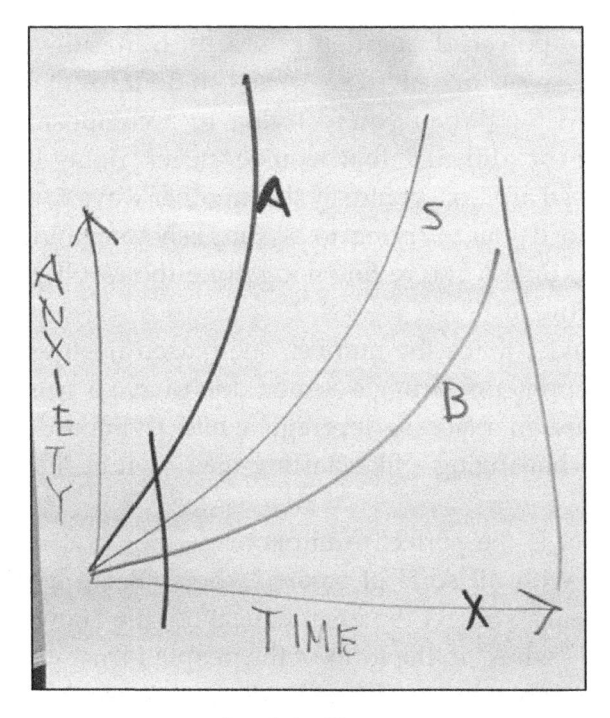

Anxiety Curve

As the Buyer (B), our anxiety naturally rises as we get more into the details of due diligence and funding. It climbs further as we approach closing and there are multiple details to manage: the lender, the title office, the management company, etc.

The Seller (S) feels heightened anxiety because their #1 question – ALWAYS – is, "Will the buyer close?" And, in the case of my Seller, with investors breathing down his neck and two previous failed escrows, the heat was on. Don't believe me? See the text exchange to further along that took place one week before the scheduled closing date.

The Seller was blowing up the Agent's phone and that of the title company. Even my lender heard about it. It happens EVERY time.

Fantastical Formulas

I had the same thing happen on an $11 million, 294-unit transaction. Size doesn't matter. It's human emotions at work.

Finally, the Agent (A) – usually, but not always – is the most anxious because they've already spent their commission (way before closing) and are imagining a deal falling through and being unable to meet the first payment on that new pool or car, etc. (Thankfully, this Agent was cool as a cucumber).

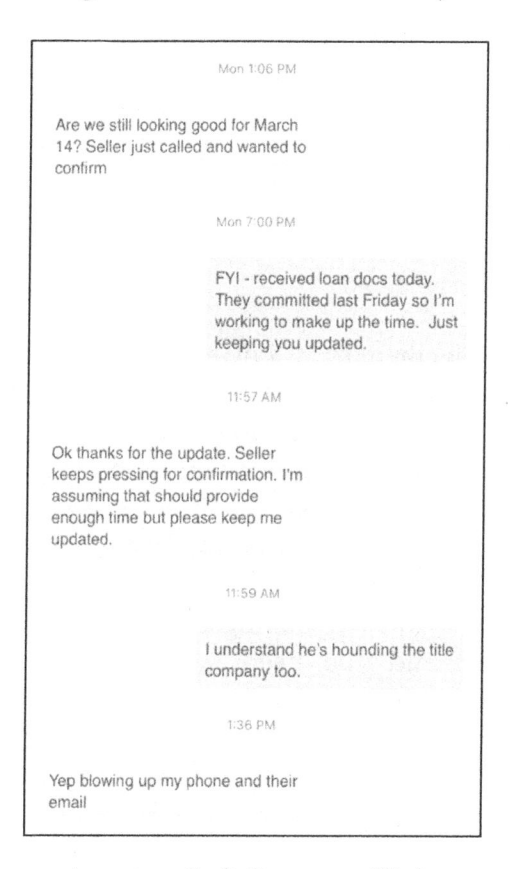

> Mon 1:06 PM
>
> Are we still looking good for March 14? Seller just called and wanted to confirm
>
> Mon 7:00 PM
>
> FYI - received loan docs today. They committed last Friday so I'm working to make up the time. Just keeping you updated.
>
> 11:57 AM
>
> Ok thanks for the update. Seller keeps pressing for confirmation. I'm assuming that should provide enough time but please keep me updated.
>
> 11:59 AM
>
> I understand he's hounding the title company too.
>
> 1:36 PM
>
> Yep blowing up my phone and their email

Agent on Left. Lance on Right

If you are looking at the scenario above, you may be wondering why you should care. After all, anxiety is the Seller's problem, right? Wrong. It really is your problem.

It's our responsibility to manage the anxiety curve of all the players, starting with our own. But it's also our responsibility to manage the anxiety of the Seller and Agent. Why? Because you might need an extension down the road. And if you've built up goodwill, you'll get it.

Wondering how you manage someone else's anxiety (especially when you're having a tough enough time managing your own)? I can answer that with one simple word – communicate.

Lesson #1: Maintain Communication

You must keep the Seller and Agent updated. Let them know of progress milestones like:

- Loan application completed
- Loan approved
- Loan docs received

If you hit a snag, let them know but also indicate what you're doing to address it. For example, notice in my text exchange with the Agent (above) where I said, "FYI – received loan docs today (Monday). They (lender) committed last Friday (i.e. they're late) so I'm working to make up the time. Just keeping you updated."

Sellers and Agents live on good news. Keep feeding it to them. The more you demonstrate that you're intently working on closing, the more goodwill you are banking. So that if you get down to the closing deadline and you need more time, you can make a withdrawal from the goodwill deposit by asking for an extension – and getting it. After all, you're closer to closing than anyone else is.

On the other hand, if you go radio-silent for 30 days with no communication and then pop up at the last minute, before closing, to announce you're not ready and need an extension, that's going to be a very difficult conversation.

Tutorial From Toledo

Let me give you an example of this with the roles reversed with the Toledo duplex I mentioned above. In this scenario, I'm the Seller. But first, a bit of background.

Fantastical Formulas

I picked up a Toledo duplex nearly two years ago from a postcard. It was a familiar story. Mom-and-pop owners had been self-managing for years and wanted out.

Note: If this describes you a small operator who just wants out – I may have a solution for you. Small apartment owners can partner with me to potentialize™ their properties. My team. My money. Shared profits.

Bonus Resource
Partner with Lance
www.AptAlchemyBook.com/Partner

The property was fully occupied with a mortgage balance of approximately $44,000 and comps of $69,000. My team offered to buy the property "subject-to" (take over payments) and the seller agreed.

I bought it with absolutely no cash. I actually got a check back at closing for the rent prorations and deposits. I left the virtual closing table with a title to a duplex, $25,000 equity and a check for $1,000 or so. My team found me a local management company and I've been collecting rent for the past couple of years. (My focus is on bigger things.)

With the recent run-up in real estate, I told my team, "Sell the duplex before something big breaks." I was actually breaking my own rule – which I teach at bootcamp. That is never own two- to four-units. Flip them.

However, the temptation of someone handing me a duplex with $25,000 equity got the best of me and I took it. Now I wanted to sell it while people were paying what I call "stupid prices." My team asked, "How much do you want for it?" I blurted out "$99,000" (wild guess) and off they went to market it.

That brings us up to present day where I received an offer for $80,000. I told my team, "Not good enough." "What do you want?" they asked. My reply, "More! Just get him on the phone and talk him up." They got him up to $88,000 (I guess they just met in the middle) and we went under contract. However, my two conditions were:

1. Show me a Verification of Down Payment (VOD); and
2. Wire $2,000 earnest money deposit (EMD) into my checking account (not the title company)

The buyer satisfied both conditions and he set closing for 30 days later.

Now, realize I had maybe one hour total time invested over the life of this project but the seller seemed shaky to me. He had the cash for the down payment, but he produced some silly hard money preapproval letter, which are all but worthless as they contain a half-dozen out clauses. Basically, anyone with a pulse can get one of these (as I teach at boot camp). The only reason I went with him was the $2,000 EMD in my account and he (and his agent) seemed really interested. By the way, I insisted he pay his agent's fee and he agreed.

Sure enough, a week before closing he asked for an extension (after going radio-silent for three weeks). My team asked if I'd grant an extension. I retorted, "Go find out how far along he is with his financing." My team got the buyer's lender on the phone and he spilled the beans. Turns out that the buyer had just made application after three weeks of doing nothing. What's more, the lender sent us the specs on the buyer's loan.

The loan specs showed the buyer was looking for a $110,000 appraisal and a $94,000 loan (recall my sales contract was only for $88,000). When I saw this, I realized we were way below market and I was unloading at too low of a price.

My formal response for an extension to closing then became, "Yes to the extension. At the original price of $99,000 and another $2,000 nonrefundable EMD for each week of extension that you need."

This was still a great deal based on the buyer's own analysis. They were buying FREE equity. They countered at $91,000 (which I declined) and then failed to close on time because they started their loan process too late. I pocketed $2,000.

What If The Buyer Had Communicated?

How would my response have differed if the buyer had communicated?

I can assure you that if they had practiced what I'm preaching here about maintaining communications with their seller (me), there would have been a different outcome for them. Recall the #1 question of every seller, "Will this buyer close?" That was the question I was asking myself. I never felt all that confident, but I took a chance on them.

If they had been more diligent in their financing process and maintained communication, demonstrating a trail of progress, I would have seen them across the finish line, and they'd have FREE equity now. But they didn't and they don't. And I've got a duplex going back on MLS now.

I made that foray into the Toledo duplex to double-emphasize Lesson #1 about maintaining communications with the seller. Now, I need to return to the 56-unit Ridgewood closing to explain the second lesson, which is...

Lesson #2: Read All Your Docs

This lesson is admittedly not as entertaining as the anxious seller or the lazy buyer, but it's probably more important. Actually, it is much more important. After 20 years, it never fails to surprise me how sloppy title companies and attorneys are when it comes to loan docs and closing docs.

Now I realize that I'm an absolute oddball. I'm one of the few people on planet Earth who actually reads every line of a contract, loan doc, closing doc, etc. You name it. I read it and as a result, I've saved myself LOTS of headaches AND money. But I also realize I'm odd in that regard and that contracts and documents can intimidate some and/or seem like Greek to others (which I admit they can be difficult to decipher).

You might say, "I just let my attorney handle that." And you absolutely have to have an attorney represent you in these transactions – starting with the purchase contract and proceeding all through closing. DO NOT SKIP THIS STEP. Yes, there is an expense but there is liability exposure here for you and this is the cheapest insurance you'll ever buy.

Note: I mentioned Legal Shield in the last chapter. I've never used them, but many clients have. I receive no compensation from Legal Shield. I'm simply sharing positive experiences from others. I think it's $39 per month and they'll assign an attorney to you for your entire transaction. Basically, Legal Shield is a lead-generating service where attorneys pay to have clients like us referred to them. There may be limits to how many pages they'll review per month, but it's still discounted rates and you can work out a deal if needed. But, again, DO NOT skip the legal review step.

Yet remember your attorney is human too and may miss something so you still have to have another set of eyes look at these docs. Attorneys review legal docs all day and I suspect their mind starts to see all contracts looking alike and they might read a paragraph and subconsciously insert language they're used to reading as they skim it.

That means, you also must read the docs or find someone else who has a high attention to detail to read them for you. My coaching and mastermind clients have access to me. I review their docs for them.

I'm not an attorney and I don't give legal advice but you can put my oddball high-attention-to-detail skills to work reviewing your contracts, loan and closing docs. I have a natural sniffer for finding goof-ups as I'm about to share. In an attempt to make document review entertaining, I'll share some examples of document bloopers from my Ridgewood closing.

Lance's Blooper Reel

Three examples (which I'll call Exhibits A, B, and C) prove my point and make my case for reviewing all docs...

Exhibit A – Loan Agreement

My lender was a bank in Kansas which subcontracted to attorneys in Oklahoma City to prepare the loan docs. Can you notice the blooper in this extract from the Loan Agreement? (I've underlined it to help). That's right, my first payment is due April 14, one month after closing but the next payment would be May 1. Two weeks later. Huh?

Payments on the Note. Monthly payments of $_____ which consists of principal and interest based on a twenty-five (25) year amortization schedule are due beginning on April 14, 2022, and shall continue on the first day of each month thereafter up to and including the Maturity Date or until paid in full.

I called my banker and pointed out the error and he immediately said, "That's wrong. Your payment should be due the 14th of each month. Or would you prefer the 1st each month?" (I stuck with the 14th of each month because I like the idea of collecting rents from which to pay the mortgage.) This detail was missed by the attorneys. I'm sure they took boilerplate language and, in a rush, made the change. But that's the point. Attorneys are human too.

Exhibit B – Settlement Statement

I received the Settlement Statement to review right before closing. I've shown the relevant extract below. Can you see the error? This error was actually to my benefit to the amount of $17,000 until I pointed it out.

That's right. The "Security Deposits" were being double credited to me. The seller completely missed it. He should read my books because he missed a number of other things in the transaction.

Security Deposits		17,100.00
Seurity Deposits		17,100.00
Tenant Prepays		11,956.74

Exhibit C – Entity Naming In Docs

This one was on the lender's attorneys AND the title company. As I teach, two weeks prior to closing, my attorney created for me a new LLC for to own the Ridgewood property and be the borrower.

I sent a standard Assignment Letter over to the title company and lender stating "ABC, LLC is assigning all of its interest to XYZ, LLC (my newly created LLC). XYZ, LLC shall take title and be the borrower." All parties acknowledged receipt. Plain Jane stuff. Done every day.

When the closing docs and loan docs came back, there was a mish-mash of ABC, LLC in some docs, XYZ, LLC in others, and even ABC, LLC and XYZ, LLC scattered throughout the same doc. That took a couple of iterations to straighten out. To the point of my frustration where I suggested – to attorneys – they globally search and replace ABC, LLC with XYZ, LLC. Jeez.

It just goes to the prove the point that we're all human (even including attorneys) and we're all stretched more than ever. So, realize this final bit of advice, which is no one cares as much about your transaction as you do.

If all these "real-life examples" get you as excited as they do me, you'll want to download my free book, How to Make Big Money in Small Apartments. This best-seller that lays out the small apartment business includes 40 case studies of how first-timers experienced success following my system.

Bonus Resource

FREE Book: How to Make Big Money in Small Apartments
www.AptAlchemyBook.com/BMSA

Bonus Resources Summary

Partner with Lance
www.AptAlchemyBook.com/Partner

FREE Book: How to Make Big Money in Small Apartments
www.AptAlchemyBook.com/BMSA

Chapter 4
Powerful Potions

"You are an alchemist; make gold of that."

–William Shakespeare

In Chapter 1, you read about the alchemical potions I planned to pour on the Oklahoma property: Serve the residents; charge service fees in exchange for value; elevate the property to market rents; eliminate wasteful expenses along the way.

In Chapter 2, we talked about formulas and laws that would allow us to handle elevating the property to market rents and eliminating wasteful expenses. That leaves serving the residents and charging service fees in exchange for value.

This task is going to take some real alchemical magic, involving creatively boosting net operating income (NOI). You'll recall that the first two laws are:

First Law of Apartment Alchemy:
$$\text{Value} = \text{NOI} / \text{Market Cap Rate}$$

Second Law of Apartment Alchemy:
$$\text{NOI} = \text{Revenue} - \text{Expenses}$$

Therefore, if you can increase revenue and lower expenses, your NOI should skyrocket, right? Just between us, the ideas behind boosting NOI are where the real science begins; the ability to look at a property and size up all the opportunities to create gold.

But I can't take all the credit for this powerful potion. I learned this insight from Jay Abraham many years ago. Now, Jay is not a real estate guy. He's a preeminent marketing genius who's worked with hundreds of different business types and industries. They call him the $7 Billion Man for the value he's created in so many types of businesses, large and small. Jay is a brilliant business growth expert.

Apartments Are Businesses

In case you're wondering, "What does business growth have to do with a 56-unit or even a five-unit apartment building?" That's what I used to think until I had my epiphany moment from working with Jay. For me, it was this, apartments are just businesses.

Once you wrap your brain around this simple point of fact, you will look at apartments as more than boxes where people live and pay rent. You will see them as businesses where the game is finding more ways to leverage the asset and serve the clients (residents) in exchange for income.

The rule to wealth creation in apartments is IDENTICAL to wealth creation in business because the First Law of Apartment Alchemy is ALSO the First Law of Business Alchemy. It is ALL the same.

First Law of Apartment/Business Alchemy:
Value = NOI / Market Cap Rate

Jay's thesis is laid out in his book, Getting Everything You Can Out of All You've Got: 21 Ways You Can Out-Think, Out-Perform, and Out-Earn the Competition. It's a paltry $13.99 on Amazon but it's worth $13.99 per word.

The primary lesson he teaches is that most of the world goes around doing the same as everyone else +/- 10%. That herd mentality yields the same mediocre results. Mediocrity is the enemy. Mediocrity is what an industrial-age education system taught us to accept as we were trained to be good employees, follow "the rules" and remain under someone else's thumb.

This is why I teach things like 12 strategies at bootcamp and 50 ways to boost NOI – to cookie-cut unique processes for break-out results, which everyday people can learn and pursue. None of this is taught in school. Most of us were simply taught to be compliant. How much would your life change if you knew how to achieve greater results from the same effort?

If you want break-out results and to take control, you just need to realize the many ways to better leverage your assets, capabilities, market, situation and relationships.

Be warned though. Once I learned and adopted Jay's philosophy, I was pretty much ruined. I could no longer look at any situation in the same way (real estate, business or people). My brain automatically started dissecting all the ways I could improve things.

I became, and am to this today, what I call "The Potentializer™." I naturally see the potential in an apartment building, in a business, in a cause or in a person, and I can "see" the ways for it to reach its true potential.

POTENTIALIZER

Those of you who know me know that phrase "true potential" means a lot to me. My 44-unit West Virginia affordable housing project laid the foundation for my Operation True Potential™ (OTP) cause and mission. Anyone who saw this blighted, 22% occupancy eyesore would never believe that within 90 days months the Mayor would attend our grand opening (even having his photo taking with me and Kim wearing his OTP hat), celebrating this clean, safe place for 44 families to call home.

Apartment Alchemy

Lance, Kim and Mayor Tom Mainella at the grand opening.

The West Virginia property is one small example of how my team, my investors and our Wealth Mastermind Network are making a small dent in the universe.

OTP's mission is to transform small multifamily communities for the better nationwide. If you'd like to see some press coverage of the properties referenced in this book and the positive reactions of neighbors and the city, click here.

Bonus Resource
Media Coverage of Lance's Projects
www.AptAlchemyBook.com/Media

Powerful Potions

Let's get back to concocting a powerful potion for the Ridgewood property. We've already seen in the First Law of Apartment Alchemy that the value of an apartment building is directly proportional to the NOI (Value = NOI / Market Cap Rate).

The conservative cap rate for Ridgewood is approximately 6.5%, cap so for every $1 increase in annual NOI, the value goes up $15.4 (1 / 6.5%)! Let me repeat that just to be sure you caught that. Every $1 yields $15. In a 6.5% cap market, we could write:

Incremental Value = 15.4 * Incremental NOI.

That's leverage! One dollar yields $15! That simple but powerful relationship is what creates your gold. It all comes down to "How do I boost the NOI?"

The Second Law of Apartment Alchemy tells us we increase NOI by either raising the revenue and/or lowering the expenses. And it is here where the science begins.

I'm a systems guy by nature so I like to systematize everything with checklists and templates. The one thing that gets me more excited than anything in this business is creating for myself, my team and you what my friend, Dan Sullivan, calls intellectual shortcuts – thinking tools…

The (In)Famous 50 Ways List

The biggest and best intellectual shortcut I could ever give you (think of it as a lifetime of Christmas present rolled into one) is this this one power-packed list: 50 Ways to Boost Your NOI.

OK, it's actually 65 ways, but I always think of the Paul Simon tune, "50 Ways to Leave Your Lover…"

In all fairness, I must give credit for the creation of this intellectual shortcut in part to my Apartment Buyers & Owners Society Mastermind. In a recent quarterly session, I challenged that group to brainstorm all the ways to boost NOI and, boy, did they deliver.

Tuck this gem away. Lock it up with your jewelry. Put it in a vault. Do not lose it. Because it is indispensable to your new

Apartment Alchemy skills. It is the "potentializer" potion you pour over your projects to reach the purest 24-karat power.

50 (Actually 65) Ways To Boost Your NOI

Ways To Increase Revenue

1. Increased marketing
2. Annual rent increases
3. Late fees
4. Bill back for water and sewer
5. Parking fees / covered parking fees
6. Laundry services
7. Add in-unit washer and dryer connections
8. Washer/dryer rentals through third-party companies
9. Decorator package rents
10. Pet-friendly pet fees
11. Storage space
12. Additional person fee
13. "Special view" fee
14. "Special location" fee
15. Trash pick-up fees
16. Application fees
17. Upgraded appliances
18. Cleaning service fee
19. Vending machine
20. Transportation service with van and driver
21. Tenant insurance
22. TV cable
23. High-speed internet
24. Month to month or weekly rental programs
25. Transfer fee from one unit to another
26. Babysitting service
27. Lifestyle center targeted to that community

Powerful Potions

28. Targeted marketing to employers with a master lease by the employer for their employees due to shortage of quality affordable housing
29. Weekly housing with ACH of paychecks
30. $500 "administration fee" instead of deposit, but resident is still responsible for conditions or report to credit bureau
31. Move-out fee
32. Tech package – download app to control HVAC, key fob, monitor
33. Car wash
34. Buy satellite cable in bulk; resell at retail
35. Early termination fee
36. Violation fines/fees
37. Microwave
38. MLM Electricity (deregulated states)
39. MLM Telecommunications
40. Affiliate income (sell renter insurance)

Ways To Decrease Expenses

1. Renegotiate maintenance service agreements like landscaping and pool
2. Requote insurance
3. Appeal property taxes
4. Resident-paid water or separate meters
5. Plug all water leaks
6. Ensure toilet valves don't hang up
7. Water conservation (low flow faucets and toilets may qualify for FMac/FnMAE green package for lower interest rates)
8. Solar panels for ABP and sell-back to utilities
9. Desert landscaping; eliminate grass with decorative granite; low water-use plants
10. Renegotiate trash service
11. Partial in-house management by long-term residents for reduced management fee
12. Service HVAC regularly to lessen wear and tear

13. Low wattage light bulbs
14. Monitor repairs (show me the broken parts which were replaced)
15. Renegotiate pest control
16. Gravel and stone under trees to replace grass and lawns
17. Efficient windows
18. Reduce ambient temp in winter in common areas and vice versa
19. Solar screens and shades on windows to reduce electric bill
20. Renegotiate management fee as you add units
21. Commercial WiFi stats on all bills paid properties and fix the temperature
22. Companies who will negotiate lower rate with utilities companies like tax protests
23. Grant programs to replace windows or HVAC
24. Solar panels with accelerated depreciation
25. Master insurance policy through a property management company

Here's an added bonus... Just prior to publishing, two WMN members shared even more entries to add to the 50 Ways list. Below, I'm sharing the ones my friend, Jay Conner, calls the real "writer-downers." (in other words, the ones I'm swiping!).

Vernon Runyan recommends:

- Amazon rental lockers
- Reserved parking for residents with spots in front of their unit
- Wirelessly monitor for leaks 24/7 using Toilet Scrooge
- Water-saving shower heads (from four gallons/minute to two gallons/minute) using tamper-proof regulators (special locking mechanism ensures residents don't switch out shower heads)

Midge Pauluk discovered an apartment complex that offers valet garbage service. For $30 per month, garbage is picked up outside your door and taken to the trash bins.

Potentializing With The 50 Ways List

The 50 Ways List is your checklist to get your brain thinking on all the ways to "potentialize" any apartment project.

For example, if you are looking to "greenlight" a deal with the Greenlight Software, keep the 50 Ways List nearby and step through each item on the list to determine how it might apply.

Remember the addition of "other income" can convert an otherwise undoable deal to a doable deal. There's no shortage of other income ideas on the list. Nearly all of the items under the "Ways to Increase Revenue" header are other income, except for the rent increases.

Everyone focuses on purchase price. But that's NOT the most important deal-making factor. What is more important is what you can do with the asset. How can you potentialize it? That's the value of the 50 Ways List.

Anyone can make money on the distressed ugly stuff. Those are no-brainers. What you're learning here is how to make money on PRETTY stuff – the 90+% occupied properties which seem to have no apparent value-add. Would you be interested in making full-price offers and still profiting? That's something I like to call "polishing the diamond." (Yes, I know, I've moved from precious metals to gemstones, but stick with me – it's worth it!)

I teach this strategy first thing, day one at my bootcamps. (If I'm willing to start off with something this powerful, that should give you an idea of the other sort of jewels I pour into the hands of my students over the three days.)

Polishing the diamond shows you how to take 100% full properties, pay asking price and still enjoy great ROIs. (How much would your apartment business be affected if you could make full-price offers?)

The foundation of the strategy is the fact that most people – including agents – look at apartments as just "boxes where you collect rent." Virtually every mom-and-pop– except you now – fails to think about, yet alone collect, other income. What a myopic view!

You now have a better viewpoint. You're a potentializer!

Practice Makes Profit

As a way to stretch those potentializer muscles, I recommend that my WMN members who have access to the Greenlight Software perform the following exercise.

Take any LoopNet apartment listing and complete the Greenlight Software at "Ask Price." Bump the "Other Income" number until you get a greenlight. Don't go crazy! Anything above, say, 10% Other Income probably isn't feasible. Once the software greenlights, you know the number you need to hit. Take your 50 Ways List and "reverse engineer" to pinpoint ways you could achieve this other income. If you feel comfortable with your numbers, go ahead make an offer.

Did that last statement scare you? Don't worry! Once you're under contract, you'll have the entire 45-day due diligence period to validate your assumptions about other income, rents, etc. You'll have time to gather third-party opinions from your management company interviews and mystery shop the competition. WMN members even have access to my opinion and those of my entire team. Use all the resources at your disposal. This is exactly the process I follow.

Not following this process will box you out of so many deals with incredible upside potential. In fact, Warren Buffett put it this way, "It's far better to buy a wonderful company at a fair price, than a fair company at a wonderful price."

The 50 Ways List is the powerful potion that creates wonderful apartment complexes. The 50 Ways actually serve your clients by bringing them greater value and people pay for value. Take #8 for example. Do you think anyone would begrudge paying extra for an in-unit washer and dryer? Would anyone, ever, say, "No, thanks. I'd rather tote my wash six miles to a laundromat, fish around in my car for quarters and then sit in the steam for four hours waiting for the machines to finish washing and drying my clothes?

To Decorate, Or Not To Decorate

Another personal favorite is #9 decorator package rents. (It will be your favorite too as soon as you see the five-year average ROI!)

Our units tend to come in two flavors: "classic" and "decorator." The decorator package is what we call our standard interior upgrade. We upgrade the interiors because we can boost the rents.

On my West Virginia project, classic rent is $600. Decorator one-bedroom rent is $700 (recently, we bumped it to $750). Here's the comparison between classic and decorator.

Classic ($600 1 BR)

- Brown carpet
- White walls
- Standard appliances

Decorator ($750 1 BR)

- Vinyl luxury laminate flooring
- Agreeable Gray walls
- Standard appliances
- Updated brushed nickel light fixtures
- New brushed nickel cabinet knobs
- Polished / stained / painted cabinets
- Resurfaced countertops

Every classic unit is the same. Every decorator unit is the same. It's cookie cutter.

We use Agreeable Gray (yes, that's the name) for the wall color because that's the most popular color you find today in model homes. Remember, you never need to hire a decorator. Just check out what's popular in the models. Let the big companies pay for the decorators.

Want to know the side-benefit of vinyl luxury laminate flooring? Yes, it looks better than carpet. Yes, it lasts longer than carpet. But the new additional benefit is it's pet resistant! It supports my pet-friendly strategy.

What few people realize is the absolutely astronomical ROI on your money from a $5,000 upgrade to an apartment that yields just a $100 rent increase.

As a matter of fact, I was telling someone recently what the ROI was, and they didn't believe me. I get it. It's higher than the 1% (or less) you're earning in your CD. So let me show you the math. It's simple and it's indisputable. It's just math. (The Greenlight Software does the calculations automatically for WMN members.)

Let's go back to the First Law of Apartment Alchemy.

$$\text{Value} = \text{NOI} / \text{Market Cap Rate}$$

The decorator package costs no more than $5,000 per unit in rehab, labor and materials to receive a $100 per month rent increase. That $100 rent bump boosts NOI, which incrementally boosts BOTH the value and the cash flow.

To compute ROI, we look at five-year average ROI, since that's the typical lifecycle of a project. Let's be ultra conservative and assume that we only receive increased rents for four out of the five years. Why? Because maybe someone already lives there when we take over and they have 11 months left on their lease, which of course we must honor as the new owner.

On that basis, here's the math...

$$\text{Increased Value} = \$100 * 12 \text{ months} / 6.5\%$$
$$= \$18,461 \text{ Equity per Unit}$$

$$\text{Increased Cash Flow} = \$100 * 12 \text{ months} * 90\% \text{ occupancy}$$
$$= \$1,080 / \text{Year per Unit}$$

Over five years, Cumulative Cash Flow = $1080 * 4 years
= $4,320 per unit

Total Return = Increased Value + Cumulative Cash Flow = $18,461 * (4 years / 5 years) + $4,320 = $19,089 per unit

5 Year ROI = Total Return / $5000 / 5 years
= $19,089 / $5000 / 5 years
= 76% per Year ROI

That is your incremental ROI on your $5,000 per door.

Don't believe it? Check the math for yourself. It's all in the incremental.

Do you "have" to do upgrades and decorator packages and all that potentializing? I know several students who balk at the idea of this type of effort because, well, it's effort. It's work.

The Lazy Person's Way To 39% Per Year

Because I'm an equal opportunity alchemist, I'll show you the lazy person's approach to 39% per year. I could show you that if you buy a stable performing and boring property in a nice area and do nothing to it, your ROI would be 39% per year using the IDEAL parameters (income, depreciation, equity, appreciation and leverage).

However, if we start with a 39% boring ROI and mate it with an incremental 76% exciting ROI from $5,000 interior updates, it's offspring is the "weighted-average ROI." Without overwhelming you with more math, I'll just give you the answer.

Let's assume I'm paying $56,000 per door and 20% down like I am at Ridgewood. (Sadly, the days of $25,000 per door are gone.) We'll ignore closing costs. So, my cash-in, per door at closing is $11,200 (20% * $56,000). I add $5,000 per door rehab to boost rents $100. My total cash-in, per door is $16,200 ($11,200 + $5,000) and my weighted average ROI on the $16,200 is 50% per year on a rehab. In other words, I get all my cash back every two years.

So, it's your choice. You can rehab or not. It's purely a lifestyle choice. If not, you enjoy 39% per year. That's great news. You can buy boring stable properties in pretty areas and get incredible returns with third-party management (but remember to "expect what you inspect").

On the other hand, if you let your management company do

simple interior updates (like mine), you can boost your ROI by 25% from 39% to 50%!

That's why the 50 Ways List is so important to your wealth creation. You want to become a master at applying as many ways as possible to always be incrementally increasing your NOI. The 50 Ways is your intellectual shortcut for ideas.

You already have the 50 Ways List. Why not join my Potentializer Club where I provide you the training while allowing you to look over my shoulder each month on how I apply the 50 Ways List to my own properties in the current market? Club membership is indispensable to the serious practitioner.

Bonus Resource
Join Lance's Potentializer Club
www.AptAlchemyBook.com/Club

By potentializing like this, you are creating great places for people to live. This is precisely the process by which apartments are being underwritten today. Don't believe me? Let me prove it to you.

If you want proof about the power and necessity of other income, just mystery shop any large Class A apartment complex. Ask the leasing agent, "What are the additional fees?"

Come prepared with a notebook and pen (maybe pack a lunch!) because the list will be lengthy: trash pick-up fee, new carpet fee, second story fee, covered parking fee, water reimbursement fee. Even with new construction, the developers load up other income to maximize their resale value.

As small apartment entrepreneurs, we leverage the fact that mom and pop don't do this. You may ask, "Why not?" That's a logical question. Here's why...

Because there's hardly a landlord training program on the planet that teaches or emphasizes what I just revealed to you. (Shhhh. Let's keep it between us.)

Landlord training programs (which you are NEVER to attend by the way; you hire it out) focus on activities like rent collections and evictions. That's obviously important but that's day-to-day operational decisions. The decisions you make are business decisions.

My new highly qualified property management company, which manages 20,000 doors nationwide, made the point on my Ridgewood acquisition. They said, "Lance, you're responsible for the strategy. We can recommend and validate your assumptions, but we take our direction from you." (That told me these guys knew their stuff.)

Expect What You Inspect

It's no different than any other business. As the entrepreneur, your primary job is to make the decisions and then keep a keen eye on performance. "Expect what you inspect."

If you don't take this tack, you are going to end up with a property that is managed like "a box that collects rent." You'll get the same mediocre results as the rest of the herd +/- 10%.

How do you think I know this?

Because I learned it from the School of Hard Knocks. In my early years, I placed too much trust in management companies. I didn't inspect. I didn't ask challenging questions. I didn't set minimum standards of performance. I assumed they knew this stuff. Wrong. Expensive lesson.

Then I learned the same lesson as I grew my training company to Inc. 5000 recognition as one of the fastest growing U.S. companies three years in a row. Whether it's my training business or my apartment business, the same business rules apply. "Expect what you inspect."

If you heed my advice gleaned from 20 years across two businesses, you'll avoid the pain of the lesson. I've already borne the pain for you. I'd hate to think this hard-earned knowledge only benefitted me.

Living The Niche Life

The biggest message of this chapter is for you to begin thinking like a potentializer about your own prospective deals. The following questions will help you brainstorm your own additions to the 50 Ways list.

- What products or services are residents already spending money on that I could switch to me and my business?
- What additional services do the residents value that I could provide for a fee?
- Where could I charge premiums for location, view, newness or amenity?
- Can I serve any "niche" resident groups that require specialized housing and charge a premium for doing so?

Does that last one have you scratching your head? Are you wondering what I mean by niche resident groups and specialized housing?

I learned the powerful specialized housing strategy from Nick Sidoti (Dr. Cash Flow) when I heard him speak at my real estate club in 2002. I bought the course – which I still have – in cassette tapes. I simply applied it to apartments where you get LOTS more leverage (more doors) compared to single family. Use the specialized housing strategy to boost your rents as well as the accompanying cash flow and value.

Here are some examples of specialized housing niches:

- Pet-friendly
- AirBNB
- Transitional Living
- Assisted Living
- Corporate Housing
- Student
- Subsidized or Supportive Housing (VASH, Section 8)

As you've probably already gathered, the pet-friendly apartment niche is one of my favorites. With pet friendly, I can collect premium rents, while potentializing and boosting the value of the properties.

AirBNB is a popular strategy, especially for properties in vacation areas. You collect premium rents by renting by the night (a variation of my "Buy Acres, Sell Lots" strategy). Several students have profited from using this strategy, but please be aware that guests post reviews (good and bad) after the fact. You'll need a system in place to tend to your guests or the negative online reviews could sink you.

Transitional living is a niche I explored in my early days of investing. Transitional living is basically halfway houses for men or women coming out of substance abuse programs. As the name says, these men and women transition back to the real world by first getting used to clean and sober living in a supportive housing environment.

Please realize I didn't operate halfway houses. I just provided the rental units – at a premium rent. In my case, I was renting to a "for-profit" group called Path to Independence (PATH). PATH leased three-bedroom units and placed bunk beds in each bedroom, housing six transitioning adults. Each bed was sublet at $100 per week. That's $600 per week gross or $2,400 per month. PATH gladly paid me premium rent because their growth depended on the supply of three-bedroom units.

Assisted living is another niche I dabbled in, which could be well worth your while. As I think everyone knows, the baby boomer population (like me and Kim and many of my readers) has driven every market trend for 70 years. First it started with diaper demand and now it's shifted to assisted living demand. We're aging.

Your specialized housing approach for assisted living is the same as transitional living. When I was looking at it, I didn't want to get into the service business of assisted living (I know nothing about it), I just wanted to be the housing provider.

So, I found an operations partner who already ran assisted living in his single-family houses. He knew all about the operations. What he didn't know was how to acquire apartments. To make it worse for him, he BELIEVED he could never buy apartments because he didn't have the cash or credit to buy an apartment building.

My agreement with him was simple. I told him, "I'll buy the property and you'll rent from me and be responsible for operations, and we'll profit share. I will have NOTHING to do with operations. But there's one condition. I'm not buying the property until we've preleased the units to clients who agree to pay $4,000 per month for the services."

I went out and found the perfect Class B 50-unit apartment in Houston and put it under contract for $30,000 per door (the good ole days) or a $1.5 million purchase price. I raised the future down payment through a commitment from the first person to sign a $4,000 per month lease.

Side note: This is a great strategy for raising private money – raise it from the people who will benefit from you starting your business (your clients). With every project or endeavor, always ask yourself, "Who will benefit more than me from my success?" Once you have the answer(s), approach those beneficiaries for support in the form of money, endorsements, tax breaks, etc.

Anyway, I was all set to close on the 50-unit assisted living apartments until the rest of the prospective clients who expressed an interest failed to sign their leases and put up their $4,000 first month's rent. Good thing I required them to buy before I bought.

That's another secret that will save your bacon – sell before you build (or buy).

Remember the old Kevin Costner movie Field of Dreams? In it, Costner's character, Ray, hears a voice tell him to build a baseball diamond with the prediction, "Build it and they will come." And naïve Ray, like a schmuck, risks foreclosure of his home in the pursuit of a whispered promise.

Fortunately, for Ray, it was Hollywood, and those fantasies can be engineered to come true. Out here in the real world, "Build it and they will come" is a surefire path to bankruptcy.

Sell First, Create Later

Instead, what we do here on the front lines of capitalism, is more logical, "Sell it before you build it." Validate your idea by getting clients to whip out a credit card or checkbook before you commit any of your own money or time.

I know whereof I speak because that's how I started by training business in 2007.

At that time, I had been investing in apartments for about five

Powerful Potions

years and thought I'd like to try my hand at teaching. One evening I gave a talk at my local real estate club. With an audience of around 100 and a flip chart and colored markers as my only visual aids, I spoke for 45 minutes on my apartment investing strategies. Just before I finished speaking, I went into my pitch.

"I'm hosting a seminar next month on how to buy apartments using none of your own cash or credit. I'm going to teach this, and this, and this. Tuition is $495, but if you sign up tonight, it's only $350."

My heart was in my throat as I nervously waited for any "takers." One person finally got up. Then two. Then four. After that the floodgates opened and audience members stormed the back table to sign up.

One week out from the class, I had 75 paying students. That's when I said to myself, "Well, I guess I better create the seminar." And the rest is history. My training business, which has yielded me and my family millions of dollars over the years, started as nothing. Simply because I insisted on selling it before I built it.

Needless to say, my first foray into assisted living didn't pan out, but it could have been an expensive and stressful situation if I hadn't stuck by my "sell before you build" policy.

Perhaps the most powerful piece of the transitional and assisted living business models is in the partnering with operators who have the know-how, but not the real estate. In fact, many of them don't believe they could ever buy the properties. Your ability to solve their growth problem by providing a small apartment building to more rapidly scale their businesses is a Godsend as far as they're concerned.

Corporate housing is similar to AirBnB in that it's short-term housing of furnished units. Your client is a company and the residents could range from blue collar pipeline workers to white collar executives. However, it merits premium rents and you generally deal with high credit renters – companies. You can even get all 12 month's rent paid upfront.

Student housing is a niche I was first exposed to back in 2008. I was buying a 40-unit property in Houston nestled between the University of Houston and Texas Southern University. I was in the due diligence phase and doing my mystery shopping.

I'd walk into surrounding apartments as a prospective renter and ask about their rents and tour their units with an aim to discover how much rent I could charge at my future property.

I pulled up to an apartment complex, overflowing with college students, and made my way to the leasing office. Upon meeting the leasing agent, I'd launch into my cover story. Here's how the exchange went...

"My daughter is going to be attending U of H next semester and I'm shopping for an apartment for her. How much is the rent for an efficiency?"

"$450."

"That's not too bad," I said.

"Sir, I want you to realize that's $450 per bed. There are two beds in an efficiency."

And that was my introduction to the "lease by the bed" strategy and the cash-flow crazy model of student housing. It is such a lucrative niche that some publicly traded companies only focus on student housing. There's that word again... FOCUS.

The large publicly traded companies generally operate in large university towns, building 160-unit apartment complexes for students. You don't want to compete with that. So, instead of large university towns, you "hit'em where they ain't." You pursue the small college towns and buy up small apartments near the campuses. Of course, COVID has kinda kicked this niche in the head but not for long. In fact, now is the time to be buying up the small apartments who lost some of their student business.

Subsidized Housing is any housing where the rent is partially or fully subsidized by the government or a nonprofit. The two largest Federal programs are VASH and Section 8. Both cater to populations who need rental assistance: low-income veterans (VA Supportive Housing, i.e. VASH) and general low-income residents (Section 8).

The advantage of subsidized housing is guaranteed payments (usually). Rent is paid via direct deposit, like clockwork. The second advantage used to be premium rents. When I got started in 2002, I'd collect HUD-approved $600 Section 8 checks for a one-bedroom BR unit when the market was $450.

Unfortunately, premium rents disappeared around 2005 or so when the Federal government shifted its emphasis (and budgets) from rental assistance to home ownership for this low-income population. A worthwhile goal, however, the process was totally mismanaged with no-doc, stated-income and neg-am loans which led to the 2008 financial crisis.

I dropped subsidized housing back in 2006 after the premium rents vanished, but when I acquired my West Virginia property (across from a college but in the middle of the pandemic), I adopted subsidized again. Today, we house a number of veterans through the VASH program. (I'm a big supporter of veterans. Four generations of my family served, including my own daughter, a former U.S. Navy officer).

Appreciate the value of what I'm revealing here. You're learning instant business models for potentializing properties. So, pick a niche. Do one. And then rinse and repeat. Stick to your niche. Perhaps you've heard the saying, "Get rich in your niche." It's true. Too many people chase everything and catch NOTHING. Avoid that with this simple three-step plan:

1. Pick a specialized housing niche. Mine is pet-friendly. I'd like to claim it was chosen after months of research, but you already know I simply had my potentializer antennae up and discovered it.
2. Test the niche. When I stumbled across the pet-friendly model at Ridgewood, we tested it on a sister property in West Virginia. Alternatively, you can test it like I did with the assisted living opportunity by preselling before committing. How do you do that? Put a property under contract. Run some "For Rent" ads in Facebook Marketplace for your respective niche. Label it "Preopening Special" so you're not accused of marketing something you can't deliver. Gauge the response. Explain to those who inquire that you're in the process of buying the property and you're preleasing. Ask, "Would you be willing to sign a lease and put up a deposit to hold a unit?" After all, haven't you seen

builders offer "Preconstruction Specials" on condos under construction? That's another example of "sell before you build."
3. Replicate, expand or modify as necessary. This is the benefit of sticking to a niche. You become better and better the more you do. That's when your potentializer skills go into overdrive. The more you potentialize the niche the more ways you find to potentialize. It's happening with me right now in the pet-friendly niche. And now it's expanding to my team – all because we are FOCUSING on it. If I was chasing Section 8, AirBnB and assisted living simultaneously, I'd just have a mess on my hands and, most likely, a failure. Go deep not wide.

Developing your potentializer mindset is key to the most powerful Apartment Alchemy. Potentializing is how wealth is created from scratch and how deals are getting underwritten today. The good old days of $25,000 per door deals are gone. Everyone is keen to grab multifamily (for all the right economic reasons) and buying on actuals won't get you into many (if any) deals. You must look at the potential in inefficiently run mom and pop apartments, not just the actuals.

Before I close out this chapter, I wanted to mention a special opportunity for you "visual learners" out there. I'm making my webinar, How Anyone Can and Should Get Started in Small Apartments, available to you as a bonus. This short online training provides a quick introduction into the small apartments business and how it can lead you to accomplish your real estate investing goals.

Bonus Resource
Webinar: How Anyone Can and Should Get Started in Small Apartments
www.AptAlchemyBook.com/Start

Bonus Resources Summary

Media Coverage of Lance's Projects
www.AptAlchemyBook.com/Media

Join Lance's Potentializer Club
www.AptAlchemyBook.com/Club

Webinar: How Anyone Can and Should Get Started in Small Apartments
www.AptAlchemyBook.com/Start

Chapter 5
Valuable Variations

"There is no heavier burden than an unfulfilled potential."

–Charles Schulz

I can only assume that the amazing alchemy presented thus far has gotten your heart racing and your creative juices flowing. However, what if you are an armchair alchemist? By that I mean, what if you are only interested in passive investing, short-term investing (wholesaling) or something else? Can you still stretch your potentializer muscles? Absolutely!

I like to call the strategies that I share here the "valuable variations." These valuable variations are for those of you who don't fit snugly in that "buy and hold" apartment entrepreneur box. I have something for everyone: passive investors, wholesalers and everyone in between.

Eight Valuable Variations (Using The 50 Ways List)

1. Investors: Evaluate deals by asking the tough questions
2. Investment Seekers: Answer the tough questions by showing your potentializer plans
3. Wholesalers: Present a compelling project

4. Apartment Entrepreneurs: Evaluate and motivate property management candidates or companies
5. Sellers: Use the list to add value and justify higher prices
6. Operators: Boost the performance of your existing properties
7. Buyers: Confidently make full-priced offers and get more deals done
8. Consultants: Position yourself as an apartment turnaround specialist

That's the great thing about being a potentializer. It's a mindset more than a method. I realize that a number of my clients are more interested in passive investing than active entrepreneurship, but you can still take these principles and profit.

If you'd like me to continue being your personal alchemist, I can absolutely do that. You can invest in my own potentializer projects right from the comfort of your home. This book has given you the "How." Now you need the "Who" to invest with. Be amongst the investors sharing in the types of returns referenced in this book.

Bonus Resource
Invest with Lance
www.AptAlchemyBook.com/Invest

Potentializing For Investors

Let's face it. Anyone – and I mean anyone – can produce a spreadsheet which will show any ROI (or IRR), given the right set of assumptions. And these days, it seems like sponsors keep increasing their ROI claims amidst competing projects. So, if you're investing in other peoples' projects, I encourage you to ask the tough questions of the sponsors, many of which are based on potentializing a project.

- What is the plan to raise rents?
- What is the plan to raise other income?
- What is the plan to reduce expenses?

Valuable Variations

- How has the plan been validated?
- What is the plan to raise occupancy?
- What marketing methods will you use?

Look for at least a few answers from the 50 Ways List to provide confidence that the sponsor's plan has been well thought out and validated. And then ask about their experience, their management company experience, their insurance coverage, etc.

Potentializing For Investment Seekers

For you active entrepreneurs out there who are looking to raise money from private investors, come prepared with answers to these questions. That's because raising private money and investing private money are two sides of the same coin. Anticipate the questions and prepare the answers in advance.

In my teaching and training career, I cover several topics. A personal favorite of mine is training individuals how to wisely invest their self-directed IRAs (SDIRAs). In preparing for a recent course, I surveyed my database of SDIRA owners and asked them, "What's your number one concern when it comes to investing your SDIRA?"

The most common response was, "How do I invest safely and minimize my risk?"

That's always the biggest concern on investors' minds. We humans have a strong tendency to preserve capital. That preservation mindset often leads individuals to never invest, which is bad too – especially in today's environment of inflation.

So, the directive is clear. Passive investors, allay that number one concern by asking the tough questions you're learning here. And, investment seekers, take that number one concern to heart and proactively address the challenging questions upfront with your potential private investors. Make a list of questions and prepare an FAQ handout.

Enumerate all the ways you intend to boost the NOI. Cite multiple plans and exit strategies. Take the entire checklist and answer those questions about your prospective deal. Structure your investment as the perfect solution to their investing needs.

Lastly, always remember that ALL private lenders want to know about the return OF their capital before you tell them about the return ON their capital.

I know it's tempting to want to keep all those potentializing profits to yourself (why pay a private lender?), but few active apartment entrepreneurs have the necessary down payments or rehab capital right in their pockets. In fact, if you're doing this right, I expect you to run out of personal capital quickly.

If it makes you feel any better, please realize you don't pay the private lender. The property pays. You put together and run the projects. Private lenders get paid from you sharing a portion of BOTH the monthly cash flow and the equity created. But they get paid first. They're "preferred."

For example, I pay 12% to 18% per year, on passive cash invested. But remember, if they are making money, I'm generally making money too. It's a beautiful thing.

So, where do you find these money partners? Why not let those SDIRA lenders I referenced earlier get in on the action? These poor folks are earning next to nothing in their accounts because they tend to keep their IRAs invested in cash. And, in the meantime, SDIRA administrative fees, combined with inflation, are eroding the purchasing power of their cash-heavy SDIRA accounts.

That means those SDIRA accounts decrease in real value each day they sit idle (and, no, SDIRA owners cannot deduct their SDIRA losses).

Therefore, your apartment endeavors are your opportunity to HELP the 95% of SDIRA account holders who earn less than 1% in the accounts. It's your duty and downright un-American for you to not be sourcing deals and making them available to your SDIRA friends, family, work, school and faith connections.

Please hurry! Washington is always looking to chip away at the Roth IRA – the choice for tax-free investments for LIFE. Why would they do that? Because the Federal government needs more tax revenue to pay the tremendous green ink bill from the printing machines in D.C.

If you happen to own an SDIRA yourself that's performing

dismally, I have an answer for you. In my special report, How to Safely Pick Winners for your Self-Directed IRA, you'll learn how to safety invest your starving self-directed IRA monies into other people's potentializer projects.

Bonus Resource
Special Report: How to Safely Pick Winners for Your Self-Directed IRA
www.AptAlchemyBook.com/SDIRA

Potentializing For Wholesalers

As for our variable variations, we've talked about passive investors using the 50 Ways List, but what about wholesalers? Does it work for them? I'm glad you asked!

Up to now, we've concentrated on using the 50 Ways List when you are going into a project. I've taught you that to compete in this market (especially with Internet or broker listings), you have to look at pro forma, other income and rent, and do it conservatively and with confidence.

But what about when selling a property, or a contract when it comes to wholesalers.

Take out that handy dandy list again. When you're selling a property or a contract, you want to promote as many additional "other income" possibilities as you can plausibly imagine and make that part of your promotional package.

For example, you put a mom-and-pop, 10-unit property under contract, which has ZERO other income. When you begin to shop it to investors, lay out a proven strategy to boost other income to 3% to 6% of gross income. See what that does to your sales value and wholesale fee spread.

In essence, take everything I just taught you about the importance of other income in boosting NOI and educate your prospective buyers on all the opportunities on your property to correct for lazy management. Sell on pro forma.

OK, let me qualify that. Sell on pro forma, but don't take it too far. How far is too far? Follow the same conservative rules of potentializing as I teach. If you believe you could achieve "X" level of improved performance, price the property based on that level of "X" performance.

Just don't go crazy. Remember that you're selling investment property and a buyer – who trusts you – will buy over and over from you, sight unseen.

Yet again, I'm going to digress with a personal story to illustrate this principle.

When I was just getting started investing in 2004, I was selling five condo units as a multifamily bundle – my first time to sell a property. I was trying to exit a bad partnership that was eating up my limited cash and credit cards. (That story is for another day.) I needed to sell those five units to dissolve the partnership and get on with my life.

I had an out-of-state buyer who was ready to buy over the phone, sight unseen. We signed a contract and I waited for him to arrange his financing. He never even came out to see the property.

While waiting, I caught wind that the Condo HOA was planning to hit the owners with a significant special assessment to fix a structural issue with the building. It was insider info that maybe five people knew about. I had a big decision to make. Do I tell the buyer or don't I?

For me, it was an easy decision. I had to tell the buyer. No question. I knew it would likely kill my sale (which I really needed), but that's just the way it was. (Did I mention I'm an Eagle Scout? A scout is trustworthy, loyal, kind… Notice trustworthy is first in the list).

I called my buyer (Joel) and explained that I had just learned privately of a planned special assessment, and I felt he needed to know. I answered his questions and, at the end of the call, he said, "Let me talk to my partner. I'll call you back later this afternoon."

He called me back as promised and what he said has stuck with me for 18 years. It would turn out to be a defining moment for me in my struggling little real estate business. As such, I can recall verbatim what Joel said.

"Lance, I spoke with my partner and first we want to say we are impressed that you told us this upfront. Not everyone would have done that. Second, we want to continue with the deal. Of course, we need to renegotiate the price, but we want to continue."

They closed that initial purchase and, as a result of their trust in me, I ultimately sold and wholesaled 72 units of property to them (and friends whom they referred) over the next couple of years. That way of doing business – in an honest and trustworthy manner – and the repeat transactions that grew from my attitude are what allowed me to escape my 20-year job in 2005, at age 45.

To further make the point, one Friday in 2005 I needed $200,000 of immediate cash to buy some property at auction that I would fix up and sell to Joel's group. Joel referred me to a friend of his and we were on the phone that afternoon. We spoke for maybe 20 minutes. I explained the opportunity and the need for the $200,000, all in time for next Tuesday's auction at the courthouse steps in Houston.

At the end of the conversation, Joel's friend said this (which I also remember verbatim), "Joel says I can trust you. And I trust Joel. Where shall I wire the money?"

By the end of that same day, I had $200,000 sitting in my business checking account. It struck me later that he never asked for a written agreement. Nothing. Just where to send the money. That's the power of trust in business.

Trust in business is everything. Until you learn that lesson, you'll start every transaction from scratch every single day. Wealth comes from repeat business and referrals. That begins with trust.

I teach at my bootcamps to make it a point to earn trust in everything you do. Every act has ramifications. Every. Single. Act. So be deliberate and disciplined. Every act is programming others subconsciously on how they view us.

For example, have you ever had an experience where someone you've known for a while has missed a call or meeting and you instantly thought, "That's not like them. I hope they're okay." That's an example of your subconscious programming as a result of that other person's consistent actions. And, their consistency in little things can be translated into their consistency in big things.

In my work life, I have a habit that if I schedule a call at 3 p.m.

with someone, I make sure their phone rings precisely at 3. With brokers, I intentionally make small promises just so I can deliver. Every promise kept is programming the other person to associate me as reliable. They can trust me to deliver. They can trust me to close. (Do the opposite and you're programming the other person to associate you as unreliable. Be intentional with your promises and disciplined with your actions.)

I used that same habit to win an $11 million project over multiple national bidders. It was David versus Goliath. And I was David. Trust is your slingshot – your competitive advantage. (As you know, most other people are all talk and getting worse with the epidemic of mediocrity.)

Potentializing For Apartment Entrepreneurs

Another valuable variation is using the 50 Ways List to evaluate and motivate your professional property management on current holdings. (You DO have professional property management, right?) They do the work, but you have to lead. Remember, as apartment alchemists, we set the strategy and the priorities and we make the decisions.

As you review the 50 Ways List, choose no more than three potentializer activities to test at any single time. Feed them to your management company in chunks – not at all once. Discuss your highest priority potentializer activity, ask for feedback and get their buy in. Assign a deadline to see results and reconvene after that deadline to evaluate the results and discuss the next activity. I make it a practice to hold 15-minute morning huddles with my management teams. Remember, expect what you inspect.

OK, confession time. I wasn't born with this wealth of knowledge. I learned the hard way. Ready for another story?

Years ago, I had a 50-unit property in the city of Houston, where I lived at the time. I had a management company and I even committed one of the units as a leasing office. I asked the management company to staff the office so that we could quickly fill the property.

Within a week, they called me all excited. "Great news, we've got

Valuable Variations

Dorothy to work on your property." "Who's Dorothy?" I asked. "Oh, Dorothy is great. She's worked with us before and the residents love her." I took the manager at his word and went to sleep that night excited to have checked the box on filling my leasing office.

Over the next few weeks and months, I noticed a drop-off in occupancy with my weekly property reports, especially in second-floor units. I asked my management company about it and they shrugged it off, "Don't worry. Dorothy will take care of it." This pattern went on for probably three months.

Finally, I'd had enough of the declining performance and decided to drive out to the property myself and inspect the situation. I met Dorothy for the first time. Lovely lady. I could understand why the residents loved her. Only one problem when it came to leasing – Dorothy couldn't climb stairs to show the second floor units.

With this discovery of my leasing problem, I was both flabbergasted and angry. Angry that my professional management company hadn't figured out the problem on their own. Especially after I asked about it repeatedly. Needless to say, I fired them. But the whole point of this side story is to again reemphasize, expect what you inspect.

Back to the subject at hand, which was assigning one to three potentializer ideas to your management company.

If the management company is good, they should buy in to improving the property and automatically contribute ideas on their own. On the other hand, if you encounter resistance or apathy, you're pushing on a rope; it's probably time to switch management companies (unless you're satisfied with mediocre performance).

If you've seen the handwriting on the wall and know you need to switch (or start using) management companies, you can even use your 50 Ways List to screen or benchmark property manager candidates.

As you know by now, choosing the right management company is a critical component to potentializing. Test their knowledge and creativity by asking, "What three things could you do to boost performance at this property?" Then, sit back and let them impress you.

If they look at you with their mouth open, next. If they start rattling off ideas from the 50 Ways List, that's good. If they suggest ideas not on the list, that's GREAT! (Please send the ideas to me to add to the list.)

I used this test on the prospective management teams I interviewed for my 56-unit Ridgewood project, during the due diligence phase. Hint: I knew I'd found the right company when I didn't even have to ask them for ideas. They offered ideas for two full days as I walked side-by-side with them for the unit-to-unit inspections. They were the textbook example of what you need in a management team: high-energy, organized thinkers and action-takers. In other words, the opposite of mediocrity.

I have to get on my soap box for a moment. Is it just me or did the COVID pandemic leave behind a new pandemic of apathy and mediocrity? No one wants to work or think. That's why properly screening management companies is becoming even more important.

Two other critical questions to ask as you interview property managers and/or management companies will be the final proof you need to know you've found a keeper. The first is, "Where do you find your rehab and maintenance crews?"

Property management companies can be infected by the mediocrity pandemic. They face the same challenges of every other business today, namely finding good employees and/or tradespeople. So, it's a valid question and one you need answered before you hitch your property and wealth to a mediocre manager who can't think their way out of a paper bag. (I refer you back to my Dorothy example as Exhibit A. That was 15 years ago. Imagine that level of mediocre management thinking in today's environment.)

The question of crew staffing will automatically weed out the individual players who do property management only as a side business and will leave standing the professional management companies with several hundred doors under management. The pros have their own crews and/or long-established relationships to insulate your apartment business from the mediocrity virus.

Valuable Variations

The second critical question? How do you source materials?

Besides stuffy noses and hacking coughs, COVID brought along with it serious supply chain issues with months of backlog for certain items. That includes all the materials needed for our unit updates like I'm doing with my decorator units. In the good ol' days, you could send someone down to Home Depot to pick up a batch of materials for a single unit. Today, you might discover that item is out and your whole project is on hold.

What should you do? Here's what we're preparing to do and what a clever property manager might suggest – order in bulk and warehouse materials.

Besides saving some money on bulk purchases, this strategy enables us to maintain the "velocity" of forced appreciation. Think about it. The sooner we boost the value, the sooner we can refinance or sell the property to harvest equity, pay investors and use the cash to buy the next potentializer project.

You've already seen how potentializing can delivery six- and seven-figure returns on apartments. This is serious money. So, don't accept mediocrity.

And, remember, you don't have to sell the property to harvest the windfall. You can refinance and pull cash out, tax-free. (It's a loan!)

Use the cash-out to buy another property (preferably) or take your spouse/significant other and/or family on a great family vacation and create memories. Whatever you want! But don't let that potential go untapped!

Note: If I still haven't convinced you to do it, there's one more option. If you have a small (or large) apartment you'd like to potentialize and boost its value but don't feel you have the time or capacity, think about becoming a part of my WMN. I'll partner with you on your property. I'll potentialize it, using my money, and we'll split the proceeds.

Bonus Resource
Partner with Lance
www.AptAlchemyBook.com/Partner

Potentializing For Sellers

Similar to wholesalers using the 50 Ways List to promote other income possibilities, sellers can use the list as a value-add to justify higher prices.

Pairing sellers and buyers is a bit like advertising yourself on dating sites. Have you ever been on Match.com? I have. Back in 2011, two years after my wife died and three years before I reconnected with Kim, I spent a short stint on Match.com. I swore then I'd write a book on those Match.com experiences. But I digress.

My point in bringing up a matchmaking site is that selling a small apartment is like what I experienced on Match.com. Everyone tends to exaggerate and embellish. I recall one woman I met whose profile picture was probably 20 years old. Or the woman who listed her occupation as lawyer on the website but once I met her, confessed she was a paralegal. Now I don't care what anyone does for a profession (that's legal) but just don't lie to me.

A recent experience with a 31-unit deal in Ohio was kind of like finding out that your blind date from Match.com just got out of prison for poisoning her husband. (You only discover this after she's downed two bottles of wine, ordered the lobster and the waiter stands by patiently with the check.)

Prior to viewing this property located near Cleveland, I had spoken to the broker, "green lighted" the deal at very near the Ask Price, had my offer accepted and gone under contract. All in the span of a week.

I saw several means of potentializing this single-room-occupancy property on paper: student housing (for medical students) or workforce housing. I was going to raise occupancy from 67% to 90%, bump the rents no less than $100, add other income and start updating the units for further rent increases. I was excited. The Greenlight Software analysis was yielding my standard $1 million net return, over five years, from this little opportunity.

I arrived the day before inspections in the little town of Ravenna, and had started talking to people about the area, the rental demand and my property. I spoke with people ranging from a random man

Valuable Variations

walking his dog to the vice president at the community bank, one block away. The market situation was lining up with my assumptions. All was looking good.

A mere eight days after going under contract, I was on site to start the due diligence inspections. It was 9 a.m. My inspector was there, as well as a plumber to scope the sewer lines of this quaint 100-year-old building. My asset managers who run my projects joined me. Both drove up from our West Virginia property to check out what we expected to be the next project.

Interestingly the broker was not there. Two residents– the "manager" and the "maintenance man" – were the only folks who showed to accompany us on our rounds. The property was basically self-managed by the owner with a couple of residents helping out. The self-management part was evidenced by the low quality of the rent roll sent me and the absence of a T12.

As I mentioned, the property was only 67% occupied. The broker attributed this to the "owner being very selective." I had my list of questions for the "manager" and question number two 2 was pretty pointed.

"You're 67% full now. What keeps this property from being 100% full?"

I'd been on-site 10 minutes and his answer made me immediately realize that I had skipped a step.

"The facilities can't handle more than 67% occupancy."

I couldn't believe what he said. "What do you mean the facility can't handle more occupancy?"

He then rattled off the following health and safety issues with the property:

- The electrical wiring is so old that if too many residents turn on a hot plate in their room, it trips the breaker. In fact, the South building had a fire in 1984 and all of that building's 100-year-old wiring was replaced. The North building hadn't been touched.
- The plumbing can't accommodate more than 67% occupancy for baths and showers.

75

- The South building can't handle any more residents because the first floor is buckling and it needs shoring up from the basement.

And that was just the beginning of the faults they mentioned. Finally, I asked, "If you had a magic wand, what would you all do?" Their response, in unison, was, "Gotta match?"

I pulled one of my asset managers aside by making a slashing motion across my neck and said, "Let's go." He readily agreed. We gathered up our inspector who had started with the basements and the electrical system and relayed to him what we had just been told and that he didn't need to continue. His response, "Yeah, that's what I'm seeing already."

I must confess I have never had a broker-listed property as misrepresented as this one. None of this had even been hinted at by the broker. During a heated call I placed about an hour later, the broker pleaded ignorance, "The seller never told us about any of this." Well, did you ever actually visit the property?

I suppose I can be angry at them for being incompetent or dishonest, but I was mostly angry with myself. Like the great President Ronald Reagan once said, "Trust but verify."

I blindly trusted a licensed broker and it cost me time and money. In hindsight, what I should have done (and what I recommend you do) is pay a local realtor $200 to "pre-visit" the property. That's a lot cheaper than assembling your team and jumping on an airplane for inspections. The realtor can take photos or, better yet, Facetime or Zoom a walk-through from their cell phone.

One good thing did come out of the trip is the Due Diligence Inspection Report Scope of Items (shared in the previous chapter). I created it the night before the inspections to show the inspector my list of expectations. (He agreed with all of them.) Use it for your future inspections.

Potentializing For Operators

Operators can use the 50 Way List to boost performance at their existing properties. Apply your new potentializer skills to increase your NOI. Stand out from the 95% who do nothing to potentialize their properties and wealth.

Potentializing For Buyers

Buyers also can confidently make full-priced offers and get more deals done. Let's face it. The rules of underwriting apartments have changed. When I started 20 years ago, the conventional wisdom on analyzing and pricing apartments was to "buy on actuals." And until the last few years, that's what I taught; it worked.

But since about three years ago, there was a shift in multifamily as the rental demand increased due to demographic shifts in baby boomers and millennials. And as this rental demand was publicized, there was an accompanying proliferation of multifamily podcasts (done to solicit investors).

With those two phenomena, the wisdom of buying on actuals was forced out the window. Sticking to the traditional buy on actuals rule led to prospective buyers getting priced out of the market and so they were forced to change the rules and the market followed. As a result, buy on actuals shifted to buy on pro forma.

You might be able to slide under the wire and still buy on actuals with direct-to-seller deals generated via direct mail but if a broker is involved, you must shift to buy on pro forma.

Want proof? Read any prospectus and study the proforma P&L for properties that are soliciting investors. You'll discover rent projections, other income projections and interest-only financing. It's how the syndicators are claiming double-digit ROIs on Class A assets. They are potentializing them. In fact, potentializing is the new rule of underwriting.

If the concept of syndication intrigues you and you'd like to try it yourself, don't go it alone. Review my training "How to Syndicate Your First 100 Doors," available as both a webinar or a special report. You'll learn how to rapidly scale your efforts in real estate investing by leveraging other people's time, talent and money while you are the mastermind behind the 50 Ways List.

Bonus Resources
Webinar: How to Syndicate Your First 100 Doors
www.AptAlchemyBook.com/100

Special Report: How to Syndicate Your First 100 Doors
www.AptAlchemyBook.com/100R

You cannot make a brokered deal work near, let alone at, the ask price today UNLESS you potentialize it – on paper – during the underwriting stage. We have to look at pro forma rents, addition of other income, finance structuring and, finally, the offer price, to make today's listed deals doable.

Three years ago, I realized the rules had shifted as I was studying the prospectuses and P&Ls of syndicated deals. As a result, I created the Greenlight Software to "up our game" on deal analysis to a rigorous three-test criteria rather than the traditional and simple cap rate-based approach. I packed the rigorous math analysis behind the curtain and simplified the analysis process to a simple redlight/greenlight signal so that "a fifth grader can pick winners."

What that means is that as you're preparing to make an offer today you need two things: 1) your calculations (Greenlight Software or pen and paper) and 2) your 50 Ways List. You have to find a reasonable way to make the deal work on paper and then use the 50 Ways to reconcile how you'll deliver on the operational assumptions in your pro forma.

Potentializing For Consultants

This brings us to the last variable variation that can get you involved in Apartment Alchemy, not as a buyer or a seller, but as a consultant. With all this knowledge (formulas, potions and more), you can position yourself as an apartment turnaround specialist.

As you might imagine, I can offer an illustration from my own experience. I learned this in 2002 when I was just getting started. If you've attended my bootcamps, you've heard the story and you've learned this strategy. It's called Partner for Profit.

Valuable Variations

With Partner for Profit, I market to apartment owners that I can purchase their property outright or I can partner with them. "I'll improve your property using my money." There are many variations to the partnering structure but basically the owner contributes the property and I contribute the money, time and action to potentialize their property. We share the proceeds from boosting the NOI and value.

As an Apartment Turnaround Specialist, you employ your 50 Ways List and you start potentializing. If you need third-party funds, raise it through private lenders. Or you can offer your potentializing skills as a service and charge consulting fees. Plenty of properties need the help.

I can tell you from personal experience that this approach is a Godsend to many small apartment owners who have a distressed property and don't have the time, money or inclination to turn it around.

My West Virginia property is a prime example. When I took over, the property had a pathetic 22% occupancy. Most of the people who lived there were drug dealers or users. If the owners tried to sell the property in its current state, they would have gotten peanuts. And they knew that. But due to health and work situations, they could no longer self manage the property. In fact, they were selling their other properties just to make the mortgage payments on this one. The property was circling the drain.

I acquired it on a Master Lease Option where I pay the owner a higher price, in the future, after I've had a chance to potentialize the property and boost the value (using my money). It's win-win for both the owner and me.

It's a third win for the city who has a drug haven removed. In just 90 days, we ran off the petty drug traffic and residents and caught the notice of the community. In fact, at our grand opening just 90 days after takeover, the mayor attended.

Finally, properties don't have to be distressed for Partner for Profit. You can offer a small apartment owner of a stable property "hands-free cash flow and wealth creation" while you potentialize their property.

Bonus Resources Summary

Invest with Lance
www.AptAlchemyBook.com/Invest

Special Report: How to Safely Pick Winners for Your Self-Directed IRA
www.AptAlchemyBook.com/SDIRA

Partner with Lance
www.AptAlchemyBook.com/Partner

Webinar: How to Syndicate Your First 100 Doors
www.AptAlchemyBook.com/100

Special Report: How to Syndicate Your First 100 Doors
www.AptAlchemyBook.com/100R

Chapter 6

Why Small Apartments Are The Ideal Investment

The Secret Niche Available to Anyone

The entire basis of this Apartment Alchemy book is the power and potential of small apartments. By now, you've probably formed a picture in your mind of what small apartments are and what they can do. But just to be absolutely, positively 100% clear, I wanted to add one final chapter so there's no doubt in anyone's mind about what you can do with small apartments. What follows is my definition of small apartments and a few (OK, several) reasons why I recommend them to experienced and aspiring real estate entrepreneurs.

Beginning At The Beginning

In 2002, my first mentor told me, "I made a lot of money in houses. But I came to realize that to meet my financial goals, I needed to shift to multifamily. Multifamily provided *bigger* numbers in a *shorter* time period."

Now, I want to pay forward what he did for me when he told me to start with small apartments. Just as he did, I'm going to explain all of the advantages and how you are qualified to get started now. You don't need cash or credit, or any prior experience.

Apartments Are The Ideal Investment

One of the first things my mentor taught me is how to evaluate different investment vehicles by the IDEAL formula, which is an acronym for the perfect investment. The perfect investment has five attributes:

- Income
- Depreciation
- Equity
- Appreciation
- Leverage

Income – The IDEAL investment generates passive income; with the key word being passive, meaning that it generates "mailbox money" without your active involvement.

Depreciation - The IDEAL investment enjoys the IRS tax benefits of depreciation. Depreciation is a "paper loss" that the IRS allows to be deducted from your active income which you pay tax on. It is possible to completely offset your income tax liability from active income by owning a sufficient amount of income-producing real estate.

Equity – The IDEAL investment has growing equity over time. Equity is the difference between the value of the property and any underlying mortgages. Increased equity comes from your residents paying down your mortgage balance thru their rent payments.

That increased equity is captured as cash when you either: 1) sell the property or 2) refinance the property with a new loan and convert the increased equity to cash (tax free) – perhaps to buy more income producing real estate.

Appreciation – The IDEAL investment increases in value over time – thru 1) market appreciation or 2) forced appreciation or 3) both. And that also translates into increased equity - which can be harvested as cash.

Why Small Apartments Are The Ideal Investment

Leverage – The final attribute of the IDEAL investment is that you can amplify its yield thru leverage, i.e. use other people's money (OPM) to purchase it.

Let's examine this IDEAL formula across four different investment vehicles to discover that a commercial income-producing property – like an apartment building – is the only vehicle that possesses all five attributes.

Comparison of Investment Vehicles				
	Apts	Business	Stocks	Bonds
Income	✓	✓	Some	✓
Depreciation	✓			
Equity	✓	✓	✓	✓
Appreciation	✓	✓	✓	Some
Leverage	✓	✓	✓	

Vehicle 1: Apartments - Let's start with the vehicle of apartments. Do they have passive income? Yes, from rents and the use of management companies. Do they offer the tax benefits of depreciation? Yes, lots. Do they contain equity? Absolutely. And it grows even if there is no appreciation, thanks to monthly mortgage balance pay-down.

Is appreciation present in apartments? Yes, thru market appreciation, forced appreciation or both. Can we purchase them thru leverage? Of course. In fact, that's a key wealth creating attribute of real estate.

Vehicle 2: Business - What about owning a business? Does a business have passive income? Yes, if it is run by managers and not by you. Does a business offer depreciation? No, not really other than the small value of depreciation on the office equipment (there is depreciation if it is a heavy industry and there's lots of physical equipment).

Does the business offer equity? Yes, if it is managed by others; it can be sold or refinanced. Does a business have appreciation? Yes, if the net profits are growing and, again, it's managed by others. Can we use leverage to buy a business? Yes, again if it has true passive income. If it's really just another form of a job by the owner, none of these latter attributes apply.

Vehicle 3: Stocks – Do stocks pay income? Yes, if the company pays a dividend. No, if not. Does a stock provide you the tax benefit of depreciation? No, that's applied to the company which sold you the shares.

Is there equity in stock? Yes, you can borrow against the value of your stock. Does a stock offer appreciation? Yes, at least you hope so. Can you leverage a stock portfolio? Yes, your brokerage company will loan you money against the value of your stock (generally limited to 50% of the value) to pull out cash or buy other stock.

Vehicle 4: Bonds – Finally, is there income from owning bonds? Yes, absolutely. That is the primary reason for their existence. Do bonds offer you depreciation tax benefits? No. Is their equity in your bonds? Yes, but it's generally fixed to your original investment amount.

Do bonds offer appreciation? Yes, they can if interest rates drop but appreciation is generally not a primary reason the everyday investor buys bonds. Can you leverage your bond portfolio and pull cash-out? No, not normally.

So, when you line them up, you see that apartments are the IDEAL investment vehicle with five ways of improving your financial position. And there's also a sixth way of utilizing apartments to generate chunks of cash: wholesaling. I've wholesaled properties from three units to nearly 300 units, as have my students.

Start With Small Apartments

Based on the above IDEAL formula, I selected apartments at the outset as my primary investment vehicle to financial independence for my family. But before you start thinking, *"Wow, I'll go do one large apartment deal and be financially free,"* let me inject some experience from mentoring thousands.

The most important thing is for you to get that critical first apartment deal done. It's all a matter of mindset. With that first deal comes confidence. And let me tell you, small apartments close faster than mid-size or large apartments, typically 30 days. When we closed our 294 unit deal, it closed in 5 months and 28 days – and it was ahead of schedule! That's too long a time for your mindset and little voice to conjure up all the reasons your first deal won't close.

Also, with small apartments, there's smaller dollar amounts involved. There's less money to raise. A single private investor can fund your purchase. And when it comes to wholesaling, there's lots of readily identified buyers of small apartments (think of all the burned-out single family landlords – they are the single largest buying group of small apartments).

For these reasons, I recommend *beginning* with small apartments. Then you can scale up to mid-size and large apartments as your confidence is cemented with that critical first deal. Or you can do lots of small apartment deals.

Definition Of Small Apartments

So how do I define small apartments? There's no official definition but here's how I define it: a small apartment is a building with 2 to 30 units. However, I need to make a clarification. Any multifamily dwelling smaller than a five-unit building is *residential* and 5+ units is *commercial*. So 2-4 unit properties (duplexes, triplexes and four-plexes) are defined as small apartments but are considered residential.

The reason for this distinction is because residential properties are valued based on *"comparable prices,"* while commercial property valuations are purely based on the property's *"financials,"* it's net operating income (NOI).

Why Is The Competition So Low?

My mentor pushed me to begin with small apartments for all of the advantages I just cited. So with all these advantages, why are there so few players in the multifamily space? There's lots of people in single family, why are there so few in multifamily?

Well, I'll tell you right now there are three prevalent, limiting beliefs - or myths - that are keeping people out of this niche and they're false beliefs. And the sooner you understand them as being false, the sooner you come to realize this is your opportunity. Those three limiting beliefs, or myths, are:

- **Myth #1**: You have to graduate from single family to multifamily
- **Myth #2**: You need big cash and credit to buy apartments
- **Myth #3**: You have to deal with tenants and toilets

These are all FALSE but I need to show you why so you realize that right now – no matter your background or experience - you are qualified to start with apartments. Once you realize that, your mind will be ready to learn how to do it. So, let's do some *myth busting*.

Busting Myth #1: Graduating From Houses

Let me explain with a story…

10 Units Versus 10 Houses

I was at a real estate club years ago when an experienced colleague greeted me. He was very experienced in houses; he bought houses, he flipped houses, he even taught people how to do houses. In the conversation, he said to me, *"Lance, my goal is to acquire 10 rental houses over the next 12 months."*

Now, in my silence, I couldn't imagine a more tortuous endeavor. First, to buy 10 houses would mean looking at probably 100 deals, then negotiating 10 deals with 10 different owners. And if you did it, you'd have to oversee 10 properties scattered all over the city. Ug. So I replied to him, *"Instead of buying 10 houses, have you considered buying two five-plexes or one 10-unit apartment?"* His reply shocked me.

Here was a person very experienced with houses; he said, *"Maybe someday I'll graduate to apartments."* And that demonstrated to me the importance of mindset in getting started in this business and the false notion that somehow there was a graduation process. Not only was his strategy flawed but he would spend far more time and money acquiring 10 houses than 10 apartment units and he'd end up with far less cash flow.

It's important to understand that there is no necessity of graduating from single family to multifamily. Rather, I recommend *beginning with multifamily*. For example, my first deal was a fourplex, which I purchased nothing down with 100% seller financing. If you're already doing houses, add small apartments now.

All right, that was limiting belief #1. Let's look at the second limiting belief that holds people back and stops them unnecessarily from getting started in apartments.

Busting Myth #2: Need Cash Or Credit

There's this lingering question: *"Don't I need big cash or credit to do apartments?"* And this is a big one for people. It's a logical question. Apartments are higher ticket items and newbies naturally believe they need to use their own financial resources to do these deals, as if they were qualifying to buy a home. Well, it's a false belief and to make this point I'm going to clarify our role in real estate.

Investor Versus Entrepreneur

Let's look at the language we use and how we are labeled. In our industry we are called what? Real estate what? Real estate *investors*, right? I am a member of a real estate *investing* association and you should be too.

But when I say the term *"investor,"* what connotation comes to mind? What does an investor have a lot of? That's right, an investor has *cash, capital or money*. Well, wait a minute. As a newbie, I'm being told I'm a real estate *investor* but I'm told to go out and do these nothing-down deals.

And what happens oftentimes is many beginning real estate investors - who have limited assets at their disposal – are out declaring themselves a real estate investor but in the back of their mind, there's a little voice that's saying, *"Hey, wait a minute, you don't have the cash to buy these properties. You don't even have the credit. You're not really a real estate investor."*

And that nagging little voice is enough to shut people down because we will never take any action which is not congruent with our identity about who we are. We're just wired that way. And so by labeling ourselves as real estate *investors*, we are actually doing more harm than good.

Now, on the other hand, let's consider the label *entrepreneur*. What does an entrepreneur look for? An entrepreneur looks for *deals, and opportunities*. We are *deal makers*.

Let's review the definition of an entrepreneur: *an entrepreneur is someone who pursues his or her vision using the time, talent and resources (i.e. cash and credit) of others*. And the key word here is *others*.

So when you look at that definition and what our job is, you see that we are not real estate investors, we are real estate *entrepreneurs*. As such, getting involved with apartments is not about your personal financial resources; it's about your ability to find the deals, find the dollars and match-make. We are matchmakers (that's why I named my website www.DealsAndDollarsClub.com). And once you understand our role, you quickly realize that it's not about your cash or credit.

Now, on to the third and final limiting belief...

Busting Myth #3: Dealing With Tenants And Toilets

I've demonstrated the power of passive income and forced appreciation from buying and holding - while revealing your role as the entrepreneur, rather than the investor. There's a third limiting belief that is holding people back falsely and that is this: *"Well, don't I have to deal with tenants and toilets? I don't want to deal with tenants and toilets."*

Do you think I want to deal with tenants and toilets? No. I wouldn't be in this business if I had to deal with tenants and toilets. And so how do you avoid dealing with tenants and toilets? You already know the answer. You're going to use property management companies.

Management Companies

When I say property management, I mean a *company*; not an individual person - not a realtor who does property management on the side. You want a management company with *systems*, comprised of *people, processes* and *technology*. If one person gets sick, the property management doesn't come to a screeching halt.

You are going to use a management company which specializes in small apartments; they manage several hundred units for multiple owners. And because your multi-unit buildings produce lots of revenue, you can afford to hire good management companies.

Asset Management Versus Property Management

The rule is: *never, never, never self-manage*. You manage the managers. Your role is *Asset Management*, not property management.

You choose and hire the property management company. They are responsible for the daily operation and reporting to you. You keep tab on their performance thru your weekly and monthly Performance Reports - just as in any business. And that's what makes small apartments truly passive income.

Recap: Advantages Of Small Apartments

That's it. You now understand:

- Apartments exclusively fit all five attributes of the IDEAL investment.
- Small apartments are perfect for either new or experienced real estate investors.
- For the same effort as single family investing, you make more money with less competition.
- You don't need any prior experience.

- You don't need your own cash or credit; you use other people's money.
- You won't deal with tenants and toilets.
- Everyday people do it nationwide today.

Chapter 7

Summary Of Resources And Offers

You've served as a worthy apprentice alchemist! Now you are ready to begin conjuring some alchemical concoctions of your own. But don't feel like you have to go it alone. We alchemists have to stick together! You'll achieve your goals faster and better with the teams and tools I've described in this book.

Take a moment to review the resources you now have at your fingertips to make magic with small apartments.

Chapter 2 Resource Recap

Lance Edwards' Wealth Mastermind Network

The Wealth Mastermind Network (WMN) is a new opportunity for real estate investing. Whereas so many get started in real estate without knowing who to work with, WMN is the one-stop-shop total solution for both first-time and experienced entrepreneurs to generate cash flow and wealth through apartments, in a scalable manner.

Through the WMN, the "greats" in apartments bring their unique capabilities to your business. WMN is a modular and customizable plug-and-play platform by which deals get done and businesses grown.

LANCE EDWARDS'
Wealth Mastermind
NETWORK

Diagram showing "YOU AS OWNER" at center, surrounded by: Training, Coaching & Mastermind; Funding & Syndication; Deal Flow Generator; Buyer-Investor Generator; Property & Asset Mgmt; Insurance; Bonus Depreciation Tax Savings; Apartments Operating System (AOS).

WMN offers you these features and benefits:

Training, Coaching and Mastermind – Training and coaching through all stages of your entrepreneurial journey with a Mastermind component for accelerated growth.

Summary Of Resources And Offers

Funding and Syndication – Whether you need traditional, private or bridge financing, for both small apartments and large, you can find it through WMN.

- Deal Flow Generator – Done-for-you (DFY) marketing services create apartment deal flow.
- Buyer-Investor Generator – DFY marketing services attract buyers or investors, including brokered marketing.
- Property and Asset Management – The process of potentializing apartments requires professional management. You'll find the best-of-the-best providers with this feature.
- Insurance – Access casualty, business income, flood insurance and more for properties at the best prices.
- Bonus Depreciation Tax Savings – Cost segregation specialists help you claim 100% bonus depreciation this year.
- Apartments Operating System (AOS) – A unique system helps you automate and scale your apartment business.
- Leverage our specialists in these key topic areas: legal, financial, taxes, 1031, bonus depreciation, exit strategies, advisors and service providers.

Chapter 3 Resource Recap

Partner with Lance
www.AptAlchemyBook.com/Partner

FREE Book: How to Make Big Money in Small Apartments
www.AptAlchemyBook.com/BMSA

Chapter 4 Resource Recap

Media Coverage of Lance's Projects
www.AptAlchemyBook.com/Media

Join Lance's Potentializer Club
www.AptAlchemyBook.com/Club

Webinar: How Anyone Can and Should Get Started in Small Apartments
www.AptAlchemyBook.com/Start

Chapter 5 Resource Recap

Invest with Lance
www.AptAlchemyBook.com/Invest

Special Report: How to Safely Pick Winners for Your Self-Directed IRA
www.AptAlchemyBook.com/SDIRA

Partner with Lance
www.AptAlchemyBook.com/Partner

Webinar: How to Syndicate Your First 100 Doors
www.AptAlchemyBook.com/100

Special Report: How to Syndicate Your First 100 Doors
www.AptAlchemyBook.com/100R

Chapter 8

About The Author

It's now been twenty years since I got started in real estate; a decision made not by grand plan but by necessity. Three months prior, and on a Friday, I came into my job of nearly seventeen years, looking forward to the weekend and feeling confident about my family's financial future. Little did I understand how that day would trigger a change of course in my life.

You see, that day saw the initiation of an unannounced series of layoffs. By noon the proverbial blood was running in the halls. There would be many Fridays like that. However, the powers that be didn't call it a "layoff."

They called it an "RIF" (Reduction in Force). I'm sure some management consultant decided that they could make layoffs sound more palatable with some catchy TLA (Three Letter Acronym). Wrong. I watched as my friends and colleagues received the tap on the shoulder and in an instant their thoughts of financial security vanished. They were staggered.

Just like me, they had been raised in a school system which taught that the formula for financial independence was, "Work hard, study hard, and get good grades."

After all, with your good grades, you get a good job. You work that good job for forty years and tuck away annual savings into your 401(k) nest egg so that you can retire at age 65.

That formula for financial security and independence was deeply programmed into my psyche. My parents taught it. My K-12 teachers taught it. My college professors taught it. My bosses reinforced it for sixteen years with promotions and raises. I suppose they even believed it. Yet, in the blink of an eye...

My Whole Foundation For Financial Security Was Shattered

I was fortunate. Very lucky. I was not RIF'ed. But that day was a defining moment in my life because on that day, at age forty, I discovered that...

The Old Rules Of Financial Independence Don't Work Anymore

From that Friday, my mind became consumed around a new and burning question, "What is my Plan B? How can I generate extra streams of income? How can I protect my family?"

That search led me to real estate and ultimately small apartments. Within a year, I had purchased my first rental: a small apartment (a fourplex) with 100% seller financing. Over the next three years, I repeated the process and bought and sold fifty properties (all using OPM, other people's money).

I had discovered my Plan B. And Plan B was soon to become Plan A as my part-time income from small apartments began replacing my job income. I discovered I could make far more money with my real estate business than my comfortable engineering job. And there was no upper limit to the income. If I wanted more cash flow, I just did more marketing.

It was a whole new world to me that NO ONE – and I mean NO ONE – had previously shown me. Not the K-12 teachers, not the college professors, nor any of my work colleagues or bosses. Each of them was simply parroting the financial plan that they had been taught in their youth.

About The Author

So, it was a total shocker to my employer when I walked into my boss' office at 9:05 a.m. on yet another Friday morning three years after that first Big RIF Day in 2002, laid my resignation letter on his desk and announced, "I quit."

Frankly, I could have left sooner but my wife was very nervous about us giving up the "security" of a job. Old belief systems are quite strong and tend to fight back when we attempt to replace them. Yet, she ultimately came around, expressed her trust in me, and we took the leap of faith together. My official last day of working for someone else was July 4, 2005 (my personal Independence Day). I've never looked back.

Despite the tough times, like the 2008-2013 Great Recession and the 2020-2022 Pandemic, I've never regretted my decision to leave that job and in fact, during every instance of economic disruption, I've always thought to myself, "Boy I'm glad I'm not stuck in that old job. Out here, on my own, I have more flexibility to act and maneuver." And I did. So...

"What's the lesson?" you ask. It's this.

Take Control Of Your Time And Money

Choose a vehicle for your financial independence plan and like Nike says, "Just Do It."

Today, my time and energy is focused on transforming lives and small multifamily communities through my Wealth Mastermind Network platform and Operation True Potential cause.

Wealth Mastermind Network (WMN) is the preeminent mastermind network and platform designed for small apartments. As the new opportunity for real estate entrepreneurs, it enables anyone to leapfrog their current financial situation via small apartments. By providing access to all the resources and the great "who's," needed in apartments, WMN is the one-stop-shop for both aspiring and experienced real estate entrepreneurs to get started and/or scale in small apartments.

Operation True Potential (OTP) is my "just cause" of transforming small multifamily communities for the better. Apartments provide a powerful profit motive for anyone to get involved in small apartments but I've learned that a profit motive combined with a just cause creates a multiplier effect in business. You're invited to join my "potentializer" movement, leveraging the resources of WMN and best practices of OTP to improve and expand workforce housing nationwide.

To learn more, visit www.LanceEdwards.com or see Chapter 7. To contact the author:

Lance Edwards
c/o First Cornerstone Group, LLC
14825 St. Mary's Lane, Ste 260
Houston, TX 77079
713-476-0102
ClientCare@fcgllc.com

Disclaimer

Specific examples, case studies, and general content within these pages do not embody the average user experience. In actuality, the "average user" consists of many individuals, some of which may purchase our service and never actually use the advice or product.

Monetary results as well as yearly income are based on a host of factors. There is no way to know how well any individual will perform, not knowing that individual's background, business sense, practices, or general work ethic. With this in mind, we cannot guarantee the results of those who have succeeded using our methods.

Readers cannot assume the results that will happen when using this program. The case studies mentioned in this collaboration do not represent or guarantee any results that have already occurred or may occur in the immediate future.

Instead, the case studies represent *what is possible*, given the advice within these pages. Since each case is so unique, reported results vary and most of the results are never actually recorded. Additional information includes pricing, market conditions, personal initiatives, and many, many other factors.

Earnings mentioned in this book are based off specific examples or estimations of what could be earned, using these methods. However, that does not mean there is any specific assurance that your figures will be the same as the figures in this book. Readers must accept the risk of disappointment.

Real estate businesses and their earnings come with their own unknown risks like any business. Therefore, making decisions based on specific examples in this book should be performed with the understanding that these results will most likely not be the same as the example provided.

Always use caution when seeking advice from professionals or those claiming to be professionals. Speak with an accountant, lawyer, or professional advisor before acting on advice provided from those individuals you do not personally know.

This disclaimer means that you agree that our company is not responsible for the success or failure of your business decisions, relating to information presented by our company, products or services. This notice refers to "you," "your," "reader," and "user," meaning "you the reader." In regards to "we" or "our," we are referring to Lance Edwards or First Cornerstone Group, LLC.